B.C.

HANDBOOK OF
STEWARDSHIP PROCEDURES

LIBRARY OF CHRISTIAN STEWARDSHIP

VOLUMES PUBLISHED

Handbook of Stewardship Procedures, by T. K. Thompson
Stewardship in Mission, by Winburn T. Thomas

VOLUMES TO BE PUBLISHED

Stewardship Illustrations, by T. K. Thompson
Christian Stewardship and Money, by Dr. Otto A. Piper

HANDBOOK OF
STEWARDSHIP
PROCEDURES

by
T. K. Thompson

Prentice-Hall, Inc., Englewood Cliffs, N. J.

Library of Congress Catalog Card Number: 64-20977
Printed in the United States of America
T 38202 (paper)   T 38203 (case)

Prentice-Hall International, Inc., *London*
Prentice-Hall of Australia, Pty., Ltd., *Sydney*
Prentice-Hall of Canada, Ltd., *Toronto*
Prentice-Hall of India (Private) Ltd., *New Delhi*
Prentice-Hall of Japan, Inc., *Tokyo*
Prentice-Hall de Mexico, S. A., *Mexico City*

CONTENTS

INTRODUCTION

LIBRARY OF CHRISTIAN STEWARDSHIP will provide the pastor and the stewardship-finance leaders of the congregation with needed background materials. This first volume, *Handbook of Stewardship Procedures*, affords a brief outline of the whole field of Christian stewardship including important source references to books, films, filmstrips and denominational literature. The succeeding volumes in the series will deal with various stewardship themes in detail. *Stewardship in Mission*, (Volume two), a symposium edited by Winburn T. Thomas, brings together a group of distinguished theologians who show that Christian stewardship must issue in a vigorous missionary activity and that mission must be based on stewardship principles. Later volumes will deal with such subjects as the Christian Meaning of Money, Stewardship Illustrations, a Stewardship Commentary on the Old Testament, a Stewardship Commentary on the New Testament, and related considerations.

All volumes in the series will be published both in cloth and paper-bound editions. Their convenient size, attractive format and reasonable price will enable the local church to obtain multiple copies for use in leadership training, group study and program development. The contributors will be recognized authorities in the subject area treated. Popularly written, each book will serve as a reliable guide and ready reference for key leaders in the congregation.

T. K. THOMPSON
General Editor

PREFACE

When Prentice-Hall asked me to serve as series editor for a "Library of Christian Stewardship," it was suggested that I prepare the first volume as an introduction to the series. This *Handbook of Stewardship Procedures* thus gives an outline for a program of Christian stewardship in the congregation. Subsequent volumes will deal with these topics in greater detail.

This book is addressed to the pastor and the members who make up the leadership core of the congregation. It represents a kind of check list by which the stewardship program of a congregation may be judged. While there are many ways of implementing these program suggestions, some kind of congregational activity ought to take place in each of the areas listed.

The format of the book has dictated an outline rather than an exhaustive treatment. Most of the value of the book will be its reference to other sources: books, films, magazines.

While I assume full responsibility for the positions expressed, I wish to thank members of the Department of Stewardship and Benevolence of the National Council of Churches who have helped in countless ways. I am indebted to the following persons for their help in specialized areas:

James Patton on the pre-budget canvass and the chapter on preaching;

William Keech, Robert Allen and Paul Strauch on Christian stewardship education;

Chester Myrom and Harl Russell on "accumulated possessions";

Arthur Byers and Malcolm Blackburn on audio-visual aids;
Martin Carlson and Luther Powell on stewardship bibliographies;
John Van Iderstine and Curtis Schumacher on capital funds;
Marvin Wilbur on the printed word;
Edwin Briggs on theological literature.

A special word of appreciation is due my secretary, Miss Ota Lee Russell, who not only typed the final manuscript, but also made many suggestions on content and editorial style.

T. K. THOMPSON

HANDBOOK OF
STEWARDSHIP PROCEDURES

1

A BIBLICAL THEOLOGY
OF STEWARDSHIP

When the National Council of the Churches of Christ in the U.S.A. was formed in 1950, its constitution contained the following definition of Christian stewardship:

> Christian stewardship is the practice of systematic and proportionate giving of time, abilities and material possessions based on the conviction that these are a trust from God, to be used in His service for the benefit of all mankind in grateful acknowledgment of Christ's redeeming love.

This definition has been under constant attack since it was first set forth by the United Stewardship Council in 1944. Most of the criticism has come at the point of limiting stewardship to giving. These critics say that stewardship is equally expressed in earning and spending, and in total living.

The word "steward" is defined in Webster's *New Collegiate Dictionary* (1953) as (1) "An officer or employee in a large family, or on a large estate, to manage the domestic concerns, supervise servants, collect rents or income, keep accounts, etc. or (2) an administrator or supervisor; a manager." Thus the word is used to translate the Greek *oikonomos*,[1] which literally

---

[1] For a detailed discussion of the use of the word *oikonomia* see *The Use of Oikonomia and Related Terms in Greek Sources to About* A.D. *100, as a Background for Patristic Applications*, by John Henry Paul Reumann, a Ph.D. thesis written at the University of Pennsylvania in 1957.

means "the administrator of a house." The three root ideas behind both the Greek and the English concepts are: (1) a responsible servant; (2) an ultimate authority; and (3) a final accounting.

The use of the term in Christian tradition is rooted not only in the Bible, but in the necessities of human language: using analogies to understand the divine-human encounter. To the more familiar figures, Father-son, Shepherd-sheep, must be added the Master-steward relationship.

The essential features of the Biblical theology of Christian stewardship may be set forth as follows:

1. *The goodness of creation* The writer of Genesis recounts how God viewed His creation: "And God saw . . . it was very good" (Genesis 1:31).[2] Christianity was born into a world of Roman law and Greek culture. The Jews had been able to resist, for the most part, the inroads of the all-pervasive Greek culture about them, but with the destruction of Jerusalem in 70 A.D. under the Roman Emperor Titus, Jewish culture was sustained only in a few isolated pockets in various parts of the Mediterranean world. From the time of the Council of Jerusalem under James (about 35 A.D.) Christianity was destined, under the leadership of the Greek-speaking Paul, to become a world religion. Christianity had to be preached in the Greek language, in Greek thought forms, to persons who had little if any of the spirit and understanding of the Old Testament. Even the New Testament itself was written in Greek, although some Aramaic documents may have preceded it. The fourth Gospel is not only written in Greek, but presents Jesus as the *logos*, the organizing principle of creation in the Greek philosophy of the first and second centuries of the Christian era.

In much Greek philosophy, especially that of Plato and his followers, there is a deprecation of material things as evil, or at least of a lower order of creation. St. Augustine, the great theologian of North Africa, brought this neo-Platonic thinking over into the main stream of Christian tradition. The Bible, on the

---

[2] All scriptural references are quoted from the *Revised Standard Version* of The Holy Bible, Copyright 1946, 1952 by the Division of Christian Education, National Council of Churches.

other hand, regards the created world as essentially good because created by God. Through the long centuries of the history of Christianity the conflict between Greek and Hebrew ideas of creation has raged. In two realms, sex and money, the battle has been sharp. The Bible is clear and powerful in its teaching: God made male and female and has entrusted to them the stewardship of parenthood. While sex may be utterly debased, as in the case of Hosea's wife, it may be the means of the highest partnership with God as seen in the Abraham-Sarah begetting of Isaac.

So also with money. God has so made the world that the supplying of physical necessities—food, clothing, shelter, material goods—is a part of the stuff of life. The exchange of goods, far from being a necessary evil, is a part of the goodness of God in His creation. Paul wrote, in the truly Hebrew-Christian tradition: "God who richly furnishes us with everything to enjoy" (I Timothy 6:17b).

2. *The subjection of creation* The Genesis writer continues "And God blessed them, and God said unto them, 'Be fruitful and multiply, and fill the earth and subdue it; and have dominion over the fish of the sea and over the birds of the air and over every living thing that moves upon the earth' " (Genesis 1:28). This account of man's dominion over the earth comes in connection with a description of man being made in the image of God. This clearly meant that man had a limited and derived dominion over a part of the earth and, to this limited degree, he reflected some of the image of his Creator. Man's dominion over the earth means that he has dominion over other men: he controls the means of production of food and the other necessities of life. Thus we see stewardship as a part of the nature of man: his being made in the image of God.

3. *The source of wealth* Moses feared the temptations of wealth as nomadic Israel became a settled agricultural people: "You shall remember the Lord your God, for it is he who gives you power to get wealth" (Deuteronomy 8:18a). Man is ever tempted to consider his wealth a result of his own cleverness. Man needs to be reminded that wealth comes from the soil—from the goodness of God in nature.

4. *The idea of covenant* The Bible can be best understood as a book of covenants. Time after time, with Adam, Noah, Abraham, Moses, and many others, God established covenants. Perhaps the Mosaic covenant is the classic: "Now therefore, if you will obey my voice and keep my covenant, you shall be my own possession among all peoples; for all the earth is mine, and you shall be to me a kingdom of priests and a holy nation" (Exodus 19:5-6a). The idea of a covenant was that God in His grace came to man as a sort of senior partner and established a contract or understanding: that a man or a nation would be especially blessed if the man or the people would fulfill the high calling which God gave. The covenant always implied that man was a steward of a precious possession entrusted by God. This idea became the basis for New Testament Christianity: God through Christ would bless all the families of the earth.

5. *The word "steward" in the Old Testament* The Hebrew language has a double word for steward: *Ashur-beth*. Literally this means, "One who is over a house." Thus Eliezer was the steward of Abraham (Genesis 15:2) and heir to Abraham's fortune until the son of promise, Isaac, was born. Perhaps the most vivid symbol of stewardship in the Old Testament is Joseph. He was a good steward in Potiphar's house. He was a good steward in the jail, and he became the chief steward over the land of Egypt.

6. *The ownership of the earth* The Bible teaches a radical doctrine of property. God alone is the ultimate owner. Men, tribes, and families have only a responsible usership. "The earth is the Lord's and the fulness thereof, the world and those who dwell therein" (Psalm 24:1). All men know that they must leave this earth and their property must pass to others. At the same time most men act as if they were going to live forever. Louis XI of France was a devout king. He gave the entire province of Boulogne to the Virgin Mary. All that he reserved for himself were the revenues therefrom! Men say they believe that the earth is the Lord's but they want to get as much of it for themselves as they can—at least the income therefrom.

7. *The purpose of God* The Bible is the story of the unfolding purpose of God. The Israelites dared to believe that

they were a chosen people, chosen to carry out God's purpose for the world. Christians have dared to believe that Jesus of Nazareth is the Messiah sent from God and that the love of God is supremely revealed in the sacrifice of Christ on the Cross. Somehow, even the Cross fits into God's purpose: through Christ's death men find eternal life. Somehow, even sinful men are called to be stewards of the mysterious purposes of God. Even the humblest goods or services can be used to 'God's glory: Peter's boat; a lad's lunch; Barnabas' farm in Cyprus; Lydia's purple dye business; Paul's pen. The purposes of God are writ large on every page of the New Testament, nowhere more powerfully than in Paul's letter to the Philippians: "That at the name of Jesus every knee should bow . . . and every tongue confess Jesus Christ is Lord, to the glory of God the Father" (Philippians 2:10-11).

8. *The word "steward" in the New Testament* The Greek New Testament has two words for steward. One, *epitropos*, means the person to whom something has been turned over—a trustee. This word occurs three times. The more important word, as we have seen, is *oikonomos*, which means house manager. This word occurs twenty times in its various forms. It is used primarily of a God-to-man relationship (with the exception of Luke 8:3). This word is the basis of our English "economics." The steward in New Testament times was usually a slave who, because of proven trustworthiness, was given a high responsibility by his master: money, property, goods, or other slaves. The basic relationship was that of accountability; the master would return after a period of time and make a reckoning. The New Testament never says, "You are a steward; therefore give to the church." It rather says, "You are a steward; therefore be a good steward of all you possess."

9. *The use of material possessions to glorify God* The New Testament is full of stories of stewardship. Perhaps the most tragic failure in stewardship was that of the rich young ruler (Luke 18:18). So also the rich farmer (Luke 12:16). Ananias and Sapphira tried to buy honor in the early church. On the other hand, Zaccheaus, who had gained his money in an unworthy fashion, became a glorious steward under the influence

of Jesus in his home. Magdalene shared precious ointment. Joseph of Arimathea shared his tomb with his Lord.

10. *The stewardship of the Gospel* In Christian teaching the fulfillment of personality is living in a joyous and loving relationship with God. Stewardship is both a means and an end. God calls men to share the good news of His love revealed in Jesus Christ. Concerning this stewardship Paul wrote: "This is how one should regard us, as servants of Christ and stewards of the mysteries of God" (I Corinthians 4:1). The Gospel is the "pearl of great price" for which a wise man will sacrifice all. It is a pearl which can be kept only if it is worn and shared. The entrustment of the Gospel to "earthen vessels" like Paul was a source of never-ending wonder to the great Apostle. Through the ages Christianity has won its battles because men have believed, lived, and shared the good news that God was in Christ reconciling the world unto Himself.

2

A STRATEGY
FOR STEWARDSHIP

Christian stewardship is the ordering of the whole of life in accordance with the will of God revealed in Jesus Christ. In the New Testament, following classic Greek usage, it refers to the individual, the family, the community, the state, the world, and, in Paul's letter to the Ephesians, to God's whole plan of creation. The congregation in its stewardship has the responsibility of ordering its life to fulfill the purposes of God for that part of His Kingdom. The church board, by whatever name, usually plans a program for the church year. This is its stewardship.

From a stewardship standpoint the Every Member Visit is the climax of the church year. This is not because raising money is the most important thing in the life of the congregation, but because an annual recommitment of the person and his purse to Jesus Christ is necessary for the growth of the Christian and the advancement of the church. The Every Member Visit is a comparatively recent development in church life. In the first decade of this century Charles S. Ward, a YMCA secretary in Grand Rapids, Michigan, developed the "intensive campaign." Its features, now commonplace, were revolutionary at the time: the training of a large number of volunteer solicitors, the call in every home or office, and the limitation of the campaign to one month or a shorter period of time. The technique was quickly adopted by the churches under the title of the "Every Member Canvass." The usual church pattern became: selecting a large number of men, training them in the program of the congregation, sending them out two-by-two, and completing the canvass within a week. New features were added in 1948— the use of the filmstrip for training and the turnover chart for the call in the home. In 1951 a professional fund-raising firm, Marts and Lundy, Inc., developed the "sector" plan of the canvass for the American Baptist Convention. Its key features were the "appraisal of the giving potential," a careful program-budget building plan, and a thorough follow-up at all levels. While the American Baptist Convention developed the "sector" plan, many other communions adapted it. It also became the official program of the stewardship committee of the Canadian Council of Churches.

The following suggestions for a strategy for stewardship are meant to be a stimulus for program planning. There is little virtue in the particular time suggested for the various events but it is highly important that these activities take place some time during the year. Every church should have a definite program of stewardship and evangelism; it must win people and money for the work of Christ.

In the course of Christian history a "church year" has developed. It is based partly on events in the Bible, partly on climate, partly on tradition. For example, no one knows what time of the year Jesus was born. The date for Christmas was set by a monk in Rome about 600 years later in an effort to Christianize and redeem the Saturnalia feast. The important thing is that Christ came. Nor is there a Biblical basis for the observance of Lent. It developed in the history of the church as a preparation for Easter and has become a prime opportunity for evangelism.

Stewardship is only one of the congregation's activities. The following outline takes into consideration other concurrent projects. Most of the suggestions require few people, except at certain peak periods. Many stewardship projects will be carried out in co-operation with other committees.

Advent   The season of God's giving of His Son, Jesus Christ, offers unusual possibilities for stewardship. Most people have a bad conscience about the foolishness that goes on around them: the tinsel, the exchange of unwanted gifts, overeating and excessive drinking, and the boredom of silly parties. They are receptive to thoughtful causes which have Christian significance. Many denominations emphasize ministerial relief at Christmas time. Many families have stopped giving "presents" to each other and have turned to cash gifts for Christian charities. The use of significant Christmas greeting cards of UNESCO, the John Milton Society for the Blind, and other worthy causes has increased. Every pastor and church leader, every individual Christian, has responsibility for restoring the season of God's Gift.

January   This is an excellent month for intensive study courses: there are no holidays or church festivals. The weather in many states is too cold for weekend trips. Farming and gardening are at a standstill. People prefer to stay indoors. With each new year, there are resolutions about self-improvement. The annual meeting of the congregation is frequently held in this month. This presents a built-in opportunity to re-examine the nature and work of the church. A wealth of good material is available for study courses:

Hatch: *Stewardship Enriches Life* (for all)
Rolston: *Stewardship in the New Testament Church* (for teachers)
Keech: *The Life I Owe* (for teachers and parents)
McRae: *Teaching Christian Stewardship* (for teachers)
McMullen: *Stewardship Unlimited* (for all)
(For more complete information see the annotated bibliography.)

February   The two months preceding Easter are harvest time in the evangelistic program of the church. The canvass organization which was enlisted and trained for stewardship in the fall can be quickly reassembled for an evangelistic visitation in the spring, or vice versa for spring canvass churches. Visitors should be selected and trained. Each denomination has instruction manuals and filmstrips available from the department of evangelism. The prospect list should include parents of church school children, pledgers to the church budget, newly arrived families, friends and neighbors of members, and all who look to the church for help. February is an excellent time for a program in Christian citizenship. Valentine Day is sometimes used for a "wills emphasis": "Give your wife a new will on Valentine Day."

March-April The evangelistic visitation should be carried out in the two weeks just preceding Ash Wednesday, the beginning of Lent. Those who express interest in joining the church should be invited to a membership class held at stated times during Lent. Teenagers will have enrolled in the membership class at the beginning of the school year, but many adults will decide for church membership only during the visitation. The visitors should be trained to present the whole work of the church as well as the opportunity for confession of faith and membership. A folder describing the special services held during Lent should be left in every home. Special problems should be noted and reported to the pastor.

Laymen should help the pastor with the membership classes. Stewardship and an explanation of the financial structure of the congregation and denomination are often given a full session in the series. The filmstrip *Seek Ye First* is the best visual tool in membership-training classes. Persons joining by transfer of letter may be encouraged to take a refresher course in membership meaning and obligations. The new member should be asked to sign a pledge at the time of joining the church. He will assume this is unimportant if stewardship is not explained.

May Immediately after joining the church new members should be put to work. Christians grow as they serve. The pastor and the stewardship committee must be ever alert to recognize the skills and interests of the people as well as the needs of the community and the world. Laymen are now recognized to be the key ministers in the decision-making places in business and politics. The pastor is a kind of assistant chaplain or coach. The primary Christian witness is in the field, forest, factory, and office. The traditional church "chores"—teaching in the Sunday school, singing in the choir, ushering on Sunday—are important, but far more creative and demanding opportunities for Christian service lie in the labor union, trade association, market place, or school classroom. "Time-and-talent" enlistment can-vasses should be imaginatively followed up so that no person who volunteers his service is disappointed, even though he may not be qualified for the type of service indicated on the talent survey.

June Graduation day for church school and day schools is the big event of June. Historically, the Christian church has been the pioneer in education at all levels. Education prepares people for the best use of their talents for God and man. A basic part of stewardship is the fulfillment of Christian voca-tion. God calls men to be reconciled with Him and to become stewards in His service to carry out His purpose of redemption for all mankind. Christian vocation no longer means (if it ever did) the professions of pastor, director of Christian education, and missionary. Twentieth-century Christianity has recaptured the ideal of the Reformation—the Christian who performs his socially useful work, making shoes or bricks, or cleaning hos-pitals, or raising children, is serving God. Indeed, as Brother Lawrence discovered, it is sometimes better to pray in the kitchen than in the chapel. June is a good time to emphasize training for Christian vocation. The books of Robert Calhoun and Edgar Carlson have many suggestions. Carlson's essay in the symposium *Stewardship in Contemporary Theology* is an excellent brief treatment of the subject.

July The church year has its rhythm: July calls to the out-of-doors. Summer conferences offer intensive periods of study, recreation, and growth in beautiful surroundings under the di-rection of skilled leaders. These conferences are of many types for all ages. Individual adult, junior high, senior high, college-age, music, missionary education, family, are among the types of camps and conferences. The number of hours available for study at a one-week conference may equal a full year's attend-ance at a one-hour church school session. Summer conferences are especially useful to city folk, who need to discover that they are as dependent upon the soil, the rain, and the wind as were their fathers. The stewardship of natural resources is an important theme for present-day Christians. *The Holy Earth* by Liberty Hyde Bailey of Cornell University is the classic discussion of the stewardship of the soil.

August During the spring and summer a small committee should be at work making plans for the congregation during the coming year. Such a committee would be asking basic questions: What is a congregation? What is the will of God for our congregation in our community? Where are we failing and where are we succeeding? What additional areas of service should we undertake next year? What activities are no longer useful? Each organization of the church should be asked to present a projected program for the coming year emphasizing the work to be done, not the dollars needed. Appropriate budget balancing can be done after a full survey of needs. By the middle of August the Every-Member-Visit Committee (which probably should not be the "program" committee) should have a clearly established calendar for the period September 1 to January 31 (events such as the Every-Member-Visit season, its preparation, execution, follow-up, and the annual meeting of the church). Much effective planning can be done in the summer months, when program pressures are lighter.

September The vacation season has meant a change of pace for most congregations. Careful preparation is necessary during the spring and summer so that the congregation may move full steam ahead after Labor Day. One of the best techniques for a rapid recovery from the summer lull is a "time-and-talents" visitation in preparation for World Communion Sunday, the first week in October. Most communions furnish materials for this observance which calls for a visit to every home in the parish. Since the church school is beginning, there are often many unfilled posts in the congregation. There are newcomers in the community. This is a good time to visit every family to secure commitments of time and talents for the work of the church and the community. This canvass serves many purposes. It uncovers new people, discloses unknown abilities, reveals latent problems, expresses the interest of the church in every person in the parish, trains visitors for the stewardship visit, builds church attendance, and gets the church moving after the summer letdown. The stewardship departments of most communions have excellent suggestions for a "time-and-talents" survey.

October The Every-Member-Visit Committee has a year-round responsibility. During the spring it assists in the training of new church members. In the summer it makes intensive preparations for the fall. At this point, October should be noted as the month when information regarding state, national, and world missions should be in the hands and minds and eyes of the whole congregation. A "church program supper" should be a feature occasion when the congregation asks itself: "What does Christ expect this church to do for the coming year?" How seriously the members face this question will largely determine the success of the stewardship program. During October the visitors will be trained and the congregation will receive a letter about the total work of the church.

November Thanksgiving is the best season for the Every Member Visit. People are grateful for the harvest, for the warmth of their homes, for the coming Christmas season. Usually the second Sunday of November is Stewardship Day. The distractions of the holidays have not yet begun yet the joys of the season are apparent. The stewardship visitation should take place on a Sunday afternoon. The goal should be a report on every prospect by 10:00 P.M. on Stewardship Sunday. A complete report to the congregation on the following Sunday will give the atmosphere of victory. A well-executed visitation is often the most exciting event of the church year.

December This calendar has thirteen months. The stewardship committee will, during December, evaluate the results of the November visitation, checking such points as: Was every prospect visited? Has the pastor received a report on special problems? What legitimate criticisms have come in? Will the resources for the new year match the program as voted by the congregation? What preparations are necessary for the annual meeting? Is a supplementary visitation necessary? What changes or improvements should be made for next year? Is our congregation growing in numbers, spirit, and in usefulness in Christ's kingdom?

From time to time the stewardship movement in North American Protestantism has joint emphases on such topics as family budgeting, tithing, wills, vocation, natural resources, education. The leaders of the congregation will watch for resources available in literature, films, conferences, and personnel on these special themes.

3

THE EVERY MEMBER VISIT

Every denomination publishes a visitation manual and necessary auxiliary materials. Readers of this handbook are urged to write their denominational stewardship office as listed in Appendix A.

Definition An Every Member Visit may be defined as a stewardship program in which every home in the parish is visited by a trained canvasser (or a team of two canvassers) who explains the work of the church, the nature of stewardship, and then secures a personal commitment from each member of the family. Various aspects of this definition will become clear in the paragraphs which follow.

Importance Church programs have a way of becoming traditional and lifeless. The Every Member Visit can easily lose impact because its methods have worn smooth like an old coin. "Easier," "better," "cheaper" ways are sought such as a "mail canvass" or a "pledge Sunday with cards signed in church," or a "phone canvass," or an "until-further-notice" continuing pledge. Such variations usually mean a 10 to 30 per cent decrease each year until it becomes necessary to return to the full visitation. A full visitation is important for the following reasons. A face-to-face interview is the most difficult yet the most satisfying and effective way of communicating the stewardship witness (or any other kind of witness or personal relationship). Training a large number of visitors will have a great impact on the congregation. The congregation expresses its concern for every family and every individual. Information on the work of the congregation and the world outreach of the church can help the prospect make a worthy commitment, but not until it is personally explained to him, with an opportunity to ask questions. Important decisions are always hard and they should be made under the most favorable conditions—in the home after thought and prayer. These are a few reasons for the Every Member Visit.

Presuppositions Before listing the essentials of the Every Member Visit we should understand its background. The goal of the Every Member Visit is that every member of the parish bring his proportionate offering each week *as an act of worship.* If Christians are to grow, they must attend worship. Worship requires the giving of self and possessions. The money offering should be proportionate to income and to the joy the worshipper has found in knowing Jesus Christ. A check sent once a year may support the church, but it does not develop the sender. The Every Member Visit is, first of all, a plan to develop stewards; it is also a way of supporting the program of the congregation. Only incidentally is it a fund-raising activity. Raising money for the church is a worthy goal, but it is less important than raising men. The "pre-budget visitation" makes this clear.

In the 1920s Dr. James Patton of the Presbyterian Church in the U.S., while a pastor in Virginia, discovered that the amount of a man's pledge had little relation to the budget of the church. Some members of his church would figure, "Now this church has 450 members and the budget is $37,800. That makes my share $84 a year. If I give $2 a week, that will put me way over average—so put me down for $104." Then he would conclude with a satisfied "Boy, that's pretty good. I thought they would hit me for a lot more than that." A man with such a sharp pencil should have been giving ten times that amount, and Dr. Patton knew it. Looking at the budget was not the right way to arrive at his proportionate responsibility or his stewardship of the entrustments which God had given him. Dr. Patton went on to develop the "pre-budget canvass" in which people were asked to give on the basis of their gratitude to God and their love for Christ, and their desire to share the Gospel. A program for the congregation and its world outreach was presented, but no dollar marks were printed beside the information items. The "pre-budget canvass" was adopted, and offerings leaped forward. Later, when Dr. Patton became Stewardship Secretary of his communion, the plan became the official policy of the Presbyterian Church in the United States.

The Christian should arrive at the amount of his pledge by looking to Christ and His Cross, by searching his own heart, and by observing his community and the world.

Money is the concrete symbol of a larger commitment. Sometimes church committees ask their pastors not to preach about money: "You preach the Gospel; we'll handle the finances." Or another version: "Do not say anything to people about money when they join the church. It may scare them off." Such attitudes betray a false separation between money and the Christian faith. Jesus said, "You cannot serve God and money." About half of Jesus' teachings were about money and possessions. The Every Member Visit is a teaching program to get people thinking straight about money (*all* their money). The "church" money is not more "holy" than the rest, but it should be a symbol of the consecration of the whole income to the service of God. (See Cowling's *Let's Think About Money* and Otto Piper's article, "That Strange Thing Money," in *Theology Today*.)

The Every Member Visit in any church requires thousands of hours and dozens of people. Such an effort might not be worth the cost if raising money was a purely mechanical matter. The Every Member Visit is a school of discipleship in which Christians learn to follow Christ more completely and joyously.

Essentials The Every Member Visit has been in use for more than fifty years, and there are many variations in the patterns. Some variety is desirable to preserve freshness and spontaneity. For precise details concerning the best type for your church, follow your denominational manual. But there are certain key steps which should be followed in any Every Member Visit.

Program The Every-Member-Visit Committee must ask questions: What is a church? What should our church be doing in the coming year? Is the program we are proposing worthy of support? How can we better serve children, youth, young couples, the retired, those with special needs? How is our congregation fulfilling its responsibility to the community, the state, the nation, the world? Does our giving to missions and benevolences witness to a Christian standard when compared with local church expenses? The building of a program should involve all the organizations in the congregation, and through the medium of a "church program supper" it ought to involve all the individual members. Program should be based not so much on cost, as on urgency from a Christian point of view. After the totaling of the pledges is completed, the exact dollar amounts can be filled in. The visitor should stress program (not budget).

Giving standard One of the most controversial aspects of the American Baptist sector program was the "appraisal procedure." It was a plan by which a large and representative committee appraised the "giving potential" of each prospective giver. Only if the prospective giver asked the amount at which he had been appraised, was he told. The appraisal was based on the question: "If this man were really interested in the work of this church for the coming year, what would his weekly pledge be?" All these "guesstimates" were then averaged and this became the individual appraisal figure. A dozen or more communions used this formula with slight variations. Usually resistance sprang up: "No one is going to tell me what I should give." In most cases the success or failure of the canvass was determined by the faithfulness with which the appraisal procedure was carried out.

Some recommended standard is necessary. Without this a good man in all sincerity might give one-fourth or one-tenth of what he should. While a dollar amount should never be given to an individual as an assessment, every prospect should be given some guidance as to how to figure his proportionate responsibility. The most commonly recommended standard is the tithe. Controversy has raged for centuries over the definition and distribution of the tithe. (See the excellent historical studies by Boyd and Constable in the bibliography.) Bishop Richard Emrich of the Episcopal Diocese of Michigan has advocated the "modern tithe": 5 per cent going to the parish and, through it, to missions and benevolences, and 5 per cent a "Christian discretionary fund," as the stewardship of the donor directs.

Most stewardship leaders in North America would agree in general with the interpretation of tithing which follows: Tithing is not a law for the Christian. It is a practice which has been found useful over the centuries. It should be entirely voluntary. (For more than a thousand years it was legally enforced in western Europe.) The tithe should be interpreted as proportionate giving beginning with 10 per cent of adjusted gross income. It should be paid before taxes because the tax structure makes provision for this. Legal interpretations of "before" or "after" taxes are foreign to the spirit of tithing, because the Christian tither is not trying to live up to a legal obligation; he is trying to arrange his giving in a responsible, systematic way. Nine per cent should not be considered "sub-Christian" nor 11 per cent "super-Christian." Christianity should not be regarded as a "higher" law which requires, say, 15 per cent, while Judaism required only 10. Christianity, as a religion of grace, still has a continuing use of the Law as a discipline. (See Brattgard's criticism of Kantonen in *God's Stewards*.) The tither regards his whole income and expenditure as a Christian stewardship. The remaining portion is also to be used to the glory of God. Tithing is not intended to buy the favor of God. Tithing brings joy and satisfaction. It has great values as a standard in the Every Member Visit.

Calendar Four months are required for a complete Every Member Visit. Only a few leaders will be working during this planning period; at the time of the Visit, about one-fourth of the congregation will be working. Each step must be carried out at the right time.

Tools Your denomination provides a complete Every Member Visit manual, together with printed materials and films. Often as many as fifteen or twenty different items are necessary: letterheads, envelopes, appeal folders, prayer cards, bulletin covers, leaflets, pledge cards, visitor instruction sheets, report forms, etc. Extreme care is necessary in ordering exact quantities. Filmstrips should be purchased to assure availability on the dates needed. Supplies should be ordered not later than a week after the EMV packet of available materials reaches the pastor. This assures adequate stocks at headquarters and adequate time for delivery. Motion pictures inspire and inform. They should be booked far in advance. (See the annotated list of stewardship films and filmstrips in Chapter 7.)

Training visitors If visitors are given no training, the call in the home will likely become a matter of picking up the pledge card with a comment something like this: "Well, this is Pledge Sunday in the church. I've come to get your card. I'm sure the same as last year is all right. Sign here. Yep. Thanks. So long."

An adequate call in the home should last twenty to thirty minutes. It should consist of greetings, getting all the family together, an explanation of the work of the church, local and world-wide, a description of the stewardship plan of the congregation, and an appeal to a larger and deeper commitment. Questions should follow. Direct answers might include the promise to get the information if it is not at hand. The prospect should reach a decision while the visitor is present. The visitor should take the signed pledge card back to the church that evening for the report meeting. Two or three visitor-training sessions are necessary. Filmstrips and role-playing are key training techniques. While the primary purpose of visitor training is the improvement of the call in the home, many congregations have reported the conversion to deep Christian commitment of visitors as the most important result of the enlistment program.

Information The EMV Committee will use a variety of channels to tell the story of the church to the prospective giver: organization announcements, sermons, bulletin inserts, church newspaper, speakers in the Sunday service, missionary speakers, cottage meetings, films, telephone brigade, "church program supper," letters, appeal folders, and most important, the visit in the home. The home visit is the only sure means of communication.

Prayer The congregation is a group of people who have been moved by the Holy Spirit to join in worship and service. Only

God can build His church. The program of the church is to do the will of God. God uses sinful men who are growing in stewardship. They can learn His will in prayer, Bible study, and meditation. They can speak His word as the Holy Spirit moves in their hearts and in the hearts of their hearers.

4

PROGRAM-BUDGET BUILDING

The stewardship committee should keep clearly in mind the relationship between the program of the congregation and the budget, which is the program stated in financial terms.

Program first The visitation should be carried out on the basis of a proposed program—what the congregation is planning to do in the coming year to fulfill its stewardship in Christ's kingdom. There is no essential relationship between the amount of a man's pledge and the amount of the congregation's budget. The donor has a right to know what the congregation proposes to do with the money he gives, but the motive for his giving should be to do the work of God, not to pay the heat and light bills.

In this chapter we shall be using the word "program-budget" to indicate both the work that is planned and the dollar amount necessary to carry on such work.

Necessity of a program-budget The Christian Church is almost two thousand years old. Most people comfortably assume that we have always had the church and always will. This is not true. Christianity has disappeared from continents, countries, and communities. The Christian Church is fighting for its life in most of the world today and nowhere is the fight more difficult, more subtle, and more dangerous than in North

America and Western Europe, where "Christendom" is tempted to become an "ethical culture institution" of a pagan society. Christian leaders at all levels need constantly to re-examine the Bible, Christian history, the present culture, and economic trends to determine what the Word of God says to this generation and what a Christian program for the congregation and the denomination is today. The prophetic judgment of Amos, Jeremiah, Jesus, and Paul is needed in every congregation, community, and nation. This may seem grandiose for a janitor, a grocer, or a bookkeeper. It was not grandiose for a shepherd, a farmer, a carpenter, or a tent maker in Apostolic times.

The program-budget is a plan for growing. No individual, congregation, or community can stand still. Growth means more than increasing the number of dollars or people. Ultimately it means greater commitment to Christ and the doing of His will in all the relationships of life. Statistical measures are always inadequate, but they are useful even in church life. Church income ought to grow at least in proportion to the general economy and probably in proportion to the "disposable discretionary income." Membership should grow at least in proportion to the general population and probably in proportion to the growth index of the community in which the congregation is located. The program-budget should increase each year.

The program-budget is a plan for orderly fund raising and fund expenditure. The experience of the past offers a check list of points of strength and of weakness, but the past should never shackle the future. "Same as last year" and "We've never done it that way before" are slogans of the backward look. A creative program-budget committee will be sensitive to unmet needs in the lives of people in the parish. Projected new services create confidence in the mind of the donor. A clearly worked out program-budget means the church is moving ahead in a creative and orderly fashion.

Establishment of the goal The average church board spends about 90 per cent of its time on heat, light, the roof, the furnace, the plumbing, the furniture-breaking kids—and keeping the expenditures down. A vestryman who would spend a hundred thousand dollars in his business after only a moment's thought will haggle in the church council meeting over a small expense item. The real business of the church council is the growth of people "in wisdom and in stature, and in favor with God and man." The program-budget should first be studied by a small committee which hears recommendations from all the committees and organizations of the church. It should then frame a co-ordinated, balanced program for presentation to the church board, after which it should be thoroughly discussed at the church program supper. The congregationally approved program-budget is then made the basis of the visitation.

Priorities Physical plant needs are so apparent they tend to obscure educational and personal needs. A leaky roof may be destroying the plaster. Anyone can see that. A worship of "success" may be destroying a semi-Christian family, but this is not so apparent. People are the stuff of churches. All else is instrumental. Priority should be given to those program events which change people's lives. The very difficulty of measuring and judging these activities should be a challenge to a sensitive program committee. Stewardship requires the best use of people, time, and money for the work of Christ.

Procedures Most communions today furnish a "program builder" booklet, which is a check list of activities (and related materials) under five major categories: world mission, pastoral ministry, worship and service, Christian education, and church building. The program builder classifies projects into "necessary," "useful," and "hopeful" ("y'gotta, y'oughta, utopia"). Proper balance between these activities is of the essence of good stewardship.

Control A good program-budget provides for regular check-ups on the work being done and the money being spent. From a bookkeeping standpoint this is relatively easy, although a great deal of paper work is required. (See Bramer, *Efficient Church Business Management*.) A good system of church bookkeeping requires at least the following records: weekly offering envelopes for each donor, a weekly "cash count," a weekly "pledge count," a quarterly report to donors, a weekly income summary, a monthly "receipts form," a monthly "disbursements form," a monthly remittance form for missions and benevolences. Each month the church board should see a "Statement of Income and Expense" for the previous month and for the year to date. The statement should include "budget to date" and "actual to date." Monthly remittance of missionary and benevolence monies saves thousands of denominational dollars in interest during the slack summer season. (See the "One-Write System" of the Cyril-Scott Company, Lancaster, Ohio, which provides a single entry for recording and notifying the donor of his quarterly and annual contributions.)

Flexibility No program-budget can meet all emergencies. A good program-budget will incorporate policies that smooth out many of these difficulties. A church should carry fire, liability, and casualty insurance. Budget difficulties are avoided by providing in advance for temporary help for secretaries, sextons and ministers. In budgeting for utilities the average costs for several seasons should be calculated. Salaries should move up each year on a regular schedule. In spite of all anticipated expenses, however, emergencies do happen. One effective way of handling them is to have a policy of up-to-date maintenance of the physical property. This means that almost any maintenance project could be put off for a year because the plant is kept in good condition. Deferred maintenance can easily become a problem if allowed to continue for more than a year.

World Christian responsibility The most serious stewardship problem facing American congregations in the mid-1960s is the lack of corporate stewardship. Individual stewardship is clearly taught and widely understood, although not widely practiced. The stewardship of the average congregation almost disappears in a haze. Corporate stewardship is the recognition of the interdependence of individual, family, congregation, and denomination in the whole Christian enterprise. Just as a child cannot be born without parents, a congregation cannot be born without participation by the larger, older fellowship of the Christian Church. This is obviously true of the new congregation which has received thousands of dollars and hundreds of hours of expert leadership from the home mission board. Virtually all the congregations established the last thirty years have received thousands of dollars in grants and loans. One "mission" church in Kansas now has more than 3,000 members. This indebtedness to the larger church is true of all congregations. The Gospel has reached the present generation of Christians only because of the faithful stewardship of parents, church school teachers, pastors, missionaries, lay preachers, Bible translators, and faithful common folk "whose hand the rod of empire might have swayed." This debt of every congregation to the pioneers who went before cannot be paid by erecting memorials of marble or glass. It can be paid only by doing in this generation what they did in theirs—by being faithful witnesses to Jesus Christ in our rapidly changing world. A hundred years ago this might have been a farmer conducting a service in an isolated rural community where the "real" preacher came only once a month. Today it is more apt to be an office manager visiting his newly arrived neighbors.

Corporate stewardship points to the fact that we live mostly in groups today: labor unions, PTAs, couples clubs, social security, hospitalization, pension funds, and the like. Most social, philanthropic, and religious work is carried on through organizations. We may not like it, but we live in the era of the "organization man." A hundred years ago a dozen families could build a church because most of the land, timber, and labor were given. Today most new churches cost between fifty and a hundred thousand dollars, and it is not uncommon for a new church to spend a half-million dollars in its first ten years. This money comes from the fellowship of larger, older congregations, fulfilling their stewardship through church extension.

The same is true in world missions. A hundred years ago a missionary could begin a preaching station and an elementary school with a few books in a grass hut. A recent missionary radio station in Addis Ababa cost more than a million dollars. The Theological Education Fund of the International Missionary Council used more than four million dollars in helping train pastors. Christian work today requires close co-operation among millions of Christians in thousands of congregations.

Yet in the face of these facts, many congregations seem to be at ease in Zion. It is easy for a congregation to build a beautiful, comfortable, modern structure, call a well-educated young pastor with three lovely children (not to mention his chic wife), listen to sermons each week on "peace of mind" or "peace of soul," give 10 per cent of the budget for those poor unfortunate people "out there somewhere," encourage people to keep up their property so the undesirable elements will not move in—and believe that it is maintaining the "Christian way of life."

What difference would a sense of corporate stewardship make in such a congregation? Many of the exterior signs might remain the same; inwardly there would be many changes. The missions and benevolence committee would adopt a principle that for every dollar spent within the parish another dollar would be sent outside. This would include a $200,000 gift for an educational building overseas to match the one that was going up locally. The pastor's sermons would point out that real blessedness comes only from commitment to a great cause. Young people would be offering themselves for the ministry, for mission service, the Peace Corps, and for Christian witness in regular business and professional occupations. A neighborhood association would work at an "open occupancy covenant" by which all people would be welcome to buy and live in the community. Discussion clubs would face real issues. Volunteers would fan out over the city to help the underprivileged. The people of the church would be different—redeemed for the world, not from the world.

The program-budget committee faces the task of making mission live. This is not easy in this day of "unified mission budgets" in which the individual makes a single pledge with no clear-cut indication of how much goes to outreach causes. Many resources are available through the stewardship offices of the denominations. (See Appendix A.) One of the basic tools is the thrilling book by James Stewart, Dean of New College, Edinburgh, *Thine Is the Kingdom*, now available in paper from many stewardship offices.

The distinction between home missions and foreign missions is no longer relevant. The whole world is a vast mission field. The congregation must accept its corporate stewardship for the entire world.

5

CHRISTIAN STEWARDSHIP
EDUCATION

Since stewardship education is a part of Christian education, it is useful to inquire, "What is Christian education?"

Adelaide Case has given one answer:

> Christian education is the effort to make available for our generation—children, young people, and adults—the accumulated treasures of Christian life and thought, in such a way that God in Christ may carry on his redemptive work in each human soul and in the common life of man.[1]

This definition may be useful provided it is understood that the experience of God's grace in giving Christ is the motivation and the criteria for judging the "accumulated treasures."

A closely related question is "What are the goals of Christian education?" In 1930 the International Council of Religious Education (now a part of the Division of Christian Education of the National Council of Churches) formulated the following as a set of objectives:

> 1. To foster in growing persons a consciousness of God as a reality in human experience, and a sense of personal relationship to Him.

[1] Quoted by Dora P. Chaplin, *Children and Religion* (New York: Charles Scribner's Sons, 1961), p. 146.

2. To develop in growing persons such an understanding and appreciation of the personality, life, and teachings of Jesus as will lead to experience of him as Saviour and Lord, loyalty to him and his cause, and manifest itself in daily life and conduct.

3. To foster in growing persons a progressive and continuous development of Christ-like character.

4. To develop in growing persons the ability and disposition to participate in and contribute constructively to the building of a social order throughout the world, embodying the ideal of the Fatherhood of God and the brotherhood of man.

5. To develop in growing persons the ability and disposition to participate in the organized society of Christians —the Church.

6. To develop in growing persons an appreciation of the meaning and importance of the Christian family, and the ability and disposition to participate in and contribute constructively to the life of this primary social group (added in 1940).

7. To lead growing persons into a Christian interpretation of life and the universe; the ability to see in it God's purpose, and plan a life philosophy built on this interpretation.

8. To effect in growing persons the assimilation of the best religious experience of the race, pre-eminently that recorded in the Bible, as effective guidance to present experience.[2]

In 1958 a commission of the National Council of Churches described the objective for young people this way:

The objective of Christian education is to help persons to be aware of God's self-disclosure and seeking love in Jesus Christ and to respond in faith and love—to the end that they may know who they are and what their human situation means, grow as sons of God rooted in the Christian community, live

[2] *Christian Education Today* (Chicago: International Council of Religious Education, 1940), p. 16.

in the Spirit of God in every relationship, fulfill their common discipleship in the world, and abide in the Christian hope.[3]

The family as the key to Christian nurture All authorities are agreed that the home is the primary influence in Christian education. Randolph Crump Miller writes:

> The way in which the family is unified is the chief factor in the integration of a child's personality. The family initiates motives, manners, prejudices, and ideals. The examples of the parents and other children have various effects on the learner. The general atmosphere of home life is a determining influence in the development of attitudes. The basic stuff of religious belief and faith is established in early home experiences.[4]

William Keech describes the family as:

> . . . the place where courage, joy, forgiveness, and love apply most intimately, and Christian standards of home management become relevant and challenging. It cannot be assumed that the church can fulfill the responsibility for Christian teaching. The family *is* the church for small children.[5]

Parents are the great teachers of stewardship. Every parental decision is based upon some standard of value. Children are sensitive to what the parents consider important. What the parents *say* has little effect. Money and time are the most obvious standards of value. The whole family should participate in decisions regarding budget and vacations and other expenditures of time and money. Many communions are undertaking a "Christian Family Money Management" program. A motion picture, *The Spenders*, is useful to begin the emphasis in the congregation. A filmstrip, *The Users*, gives direction on the actual building of a Christian family budget, along with a *Handbook for the Christian Family and Money Management*. A book by David Graybeal, *The Christian Family and Its*

---

[3] The Objective of Christian Education for Senior High Young People (New York: National Council of Churches, 1958), pp. 14-15.
[4] Education for Christian Living, 2nd ed. (Englewood Cliffs, N. J.: Prentice-Hall, Inc., 1963), p. 99.
[5] *The Life I Owe* (Philadelphia: Judson Press, 1963), p. 49.

Money, is useful as a background discussion guide for a couples club or adult Bible class. These family budget materials are also useful in marriage counseling classes.

Stewardship in the church school Glenn McRae has written a useful text for the teacher or church school superintendent, entitled *Teaching Christian Stewardship.* William Keech's book, *The Life I Owe,* is useful to teachers and parents alike. In church school materials the trend has been to incorporate stewardship and missionary education directly into the basic curriculum. While this is a splendid ideal, it has not always been successful. Stewardship has often been interpreted so broadly as to include everything under "responsibility" or "commitment." For this reason the church school teacher or officer does well to exercise initiative in the use of offering meditations, special offerings, missionary visitors, Friendship Press publications, youth stewardship projects, and other tools in training children and youth in the principle and practice of Christian stewardship. The vacation church school and the summer conferences are opportunities for intensive stewardship projects.

Youth stewardship Teenagers are specially interested in three aspects of stewardship: finding a life partner, deciding on a career, and having a good time.

Sex is a stewardship in which God calls man to share in the continuance of life. It can be holy or debased, exploited or held in trust. Finding a life partner is one of the most important decisions of life. Young people know this. The building of a Christian home is the classic meaning of stewardship—"housekeeping" or "homemaking." Even Xenophon, four hundred years before Christ, had some feeling for the basic religious nature of marriage. (See Xenophon, *Memorabilia and Oeconomicus,* the Loeb Classical Library.)

While deciding on a career has become more difficult in our day because of the increased pressure to make money, young people are still idealistic. More than three thousand have served in the Peace Corps. The newly rediscovered fact that God may call to service in business and the professions has great appeal to youth. Many practicing physicians, dentists, and engineers are giving short-term service overseas as a part of their Christian vocation.

Thoughtful youth today are "having a good time" while exercising their stewardship. Several thousand German youths have given a year of service in one of the church's institutions or projects. A caravan of youth spent their 1963 Christmas holiday driving truckloads of used clothing to the needy in eastern Kentucky coalfields.

Teenagers spend about twelve billion dollars a year, according to the editors of *Seventeen* magazine. A stewardship crisis for the young person is the first paycheck. Proportionate giving should begin when the child gets an allowance for the first time, and it should never end.

The United Presbyterian Church, U.S.A., has had the longest experience with youth stewardship projects. The Reverend Robert Allen, Director of Youth Stewardship, is anxious to correspond with people interested in this field.[6]

Special projects Stewardship lends itself to a wide variety of educational projects. The United Church of Christ for many years has sponsored a "poster and essay contest," which recently has been widened to include poetry.[7] Dr. Curtis Schumacher of the same communion has successfully used a radio "spot announcement" project on stewardship in connection with his capital funds work. Care must be exercised in money-raising events with children and youth, lest exploitation rather than education be the result.

Adult education The church has been ahead of the procession in discovering the continuing education of adults. New informal Bible study groups are found in almost every congregation. Couples clubs have developed widely. The bibliography in this book contains many suggestions for study. McLelland's *The Other Six Days* is useful for discovering ways of witness in and through the vocations. Single women will find

[6] Address inquiries to him at: 475 Riverside Drive, New York, N. Y. 10027.
[7] For details, write: The Reverend Paul Strauch, Secretary of Stewardship Education, 1505 Race Street, Philadelphia, Penna.

Helen Wallace's *Stewardship for Today's Woman* helpful. The large number of unmarried adults in today's parishes requires special thought.

Membership classes Both youth and adult membership classes need stewardship instruction. Such a program should include the Biblical doctrine of stewardship, the place of proportionate giving, giving as an act of worship, the stewardship tradition and plan of the particular congregation, the missionary and benevolence outreach of the congregation, the mission fields, the ecumenical movement, and the Christian witness in daily life. A commitment card for a weekly gift to the church should be signed at or before formal reception into membership. People want to know their financial responsibility before they join an organization. The filmstrips "Seek Ye First" and "Reason for Being" give a clear presentation of the meaning of stewardship for membership classes.

The Every Member Visit Education is something that continues in every moment of life, in the church and out. The Every Member Visit is a good example. While the primary purpose of the stewardship visit may seem to be to raise the budget, actually it is a dynamic educational enterprise. The visitors learn the work of the church, the meaning of stewardship, the nature of the call, the outreach of the congregation, and the needs of the community and the world. Ideally, most of the prospects learn these things too. The stewardship visit is one of the great educational opportunities of the church year.

6

THE STEWARDSHIP
OF ACCUMULATED POSSESSIONS

I had not been in my first parish long before I discovered that leadership in helping people with the stewardship of accumulated possessions was a part of my job. In one case there was a ninety-year-old schoolteacher who had inherited a small fortune from her brother. She was planning to leave her money to some distant cousins in New Zealand whom she had never seen, on the basis of their being her "next of kin." At the same time, she was deeply interested in medical missions in India, and when she made her will, while giving recognition to friends and relatives, the major portion of her estate went for mission work. In another case an elderly widow lived so frugally that I, as her pastor, was concerned about her having enough to eat. A banker in the congregation assured me that modesty in living and generosity in giving were the basic principles of her philosophy of Christian stewardship. She made a bequest of $10,000 for the equipment of the new educational building of the church.

In the "Protestant ethic" of industry, simplicity, and saving, which continues to influence the business practices of the American people, it is assumed that responsible Christians will live within their incomes and will accumulate some savings for the rainy day. Thus, for centuries, Protestant countries have had adequate capital to finance business undertakings. The reasonable expectation is that the average Protestant family will approach the sunset years with a few thousand dollars in property, savings, or other kinds of assets. The question of "capital" giving in contrast to "current" giving comes to the fore. Every Christian will make his weekly Sunday morning offering an act of worship, drawing the money from his current income. Sometimes, however, as in the case of a building-fund campaign, he may want to make a large cash gift outright or a pledge over a year or two on a weekly basis that would exceed what could be considered a "current" gift. This is known as a "capital" gift, more out of reserves than out of income, although it may actually be a mixture of both. While current giving is expected from all Christians, the larger capital gift is more typical of people of advanced years.

The will, the basic form of capital giving Probably the earliest legal form is the will. Many papyrus wills have been discovered in the sands of Egypt. The orderly transfer of property is one of the important criteria of an advanced culture like that of Egypt. All men know they must die. A properly executed will is a part of the fulfillment of the citizen's responsibilities for his family and for society. In one sense a man must give away all that he has when making a will; in another sense he does not "give" at all, for he does not have the option of keeping. Whatever a man's assets, he must make a final capital gift at the time of his death. If he does not make a will, the state (or society) must make one for him through inheritance laws or traditions. Since the law will seldom, if ever, dispose of his property in the way he might wish, the citizen-steward should see his attorney and have a will drawn which reflects his values and which conforms to the laws of his state. Any person twenty-one years of age or over, who has assets of a thousand dollars or more, should have a will.

For the Christian the making of a will is the climactic act of a life of stewardship. Throughout the Bible life is described as a stewardship in which God is the ultimate owner of the earth and everything on it. Man is a steward whose highest calling is to do the will of God, first revealed in the covenants to Adam,

Noah, Abraham, and Moses, and revealed supremely in the life, death, and resurrection of Jesus Christ. Accountability, the Bible teaches, is of the essence of stewardship: the Owner may call for an accounting at any time. Every decision (Greek: *crisis*) is a kind of judgment, but there will be in addition a final judgment when every man must give an account of his stewardship. While the Greek word for stewardship is based on economic affairs, it really means the ordering of the whole of life in accordance with the will of God. The last will and testament, then, is, in effect, a report to God on what the steward has done with the entrustments placed in his hands by his Creator and Redeemer.

One of the surprises I experienced in updating my own will was the demand of my attorney that I "make proper disposition" of my three children—that is, to provide for a legal guardian in the event of the death of both parents. Thus the family itself is one of God's entrustments. Some years ago a group of national stewardship leaders from various Protestant denominations were discussing the question "Which comes first in the making of a will—the family or the church?" After vigorous debate, a unanimous decision was reached: the family comes first. The reasoning ran as follows: God gives men many entrustments—life, time, talents, and above all, the knowledge of His own love in Jesus Christ. One of the great entrustments is the stewardship of parenthood. Every father is a priest of God before his children. His responsibility to his family is his highest responsibility under God's providence. This stewardship may be abused so that a husband may worship his wife or a father a son (as perhaps Abraham feared he was doing with Isaac). The wise parent realizes fully that it is hard to know exactly where loving concern spills over into idolatry. In the making of a will, family responsibilities are the first concern of the Christian steward.

When family and personal debts and expenses are provided for, the Christian steward then faces the possibility of giving some portion of his goods for the work of Christ. A will is always a possible source of controversy among the survivors because the law provides a means of distribution to the next of kin when bequests are not clearly drawn. This has led many congregations to avoid having a "wills emphasis." This is a shortsighted policy, however, because much of the great Christian work of the centuries has been made possible by legacies. Dr. W. K. Jordan of Harvard University has written a three-volume history of philanthropy in England which shows that the philanthropic bequest was the basic channel for the fulfillment of Christian stewardship in the culture of England. The United States of America continues the cultural and legal tradition of the mother country at this point.

Another reason frequently cited for not having a wills program is the problem of endowments in the congregation. Many cases can be cited in Europe and North America to show that endowments tend to undercut the support from the living in the average congregation. While there are notable exceptions in some of the larger cities, endowments can be a curse rather than a blessing for most congregations. A sound principle is: if the congregation has a missionary responsibility in its parish which goes far beyond the normal expectation of support from parishioners, then endowments for that portion of the program are in order. Local officers of the congregation are wise when they encourage their people to remember the wider world of church boards and agencies: colleges, hospitals, mission boards, and the like. These groups have well-organized offices for the proper administration of bequests and legacies.

When a congregation undertakes a wills emphasis as a part of its stewardship program, the members will soon discover that, while a will is necessary in every case, there are great advantages in "giving while living." The most obvious is that the giver can see the good his gift is doing while he is still alive. A few years ago I attended a luncheon in honor of a restaurateur in San Francisco who had made a lifetime hobby of helping refugees resettle in the United States; as of that morning he had helped 5,007. A wealthy man, yes, but one who had more fun in giving than in getting. Another reason for giving while living is the tax structure. The law, by intent, encourages giving to philanthropic institutions. Inheritance taxes are steeply graduated, so that the philanthropic dollar given during one's lifetime is often greater than that same dollar if given through a bequest. There is a wide variety of patterns of "giving while living."

The gift annuity This is one of the most useful forms of giving while living. A few months ago, at the age of seventy, a certain Miss Y of Denver retired from her job as secretary in a large business firm. She had lived simply and for the last thirty years had put her savings in a mutual fund. Much to her surprise, when she figured her capital assets, she discovered that she had almost twice as much money as she thought she had. Stock splits had made the difference. In talking with her lawyer on how she could best handle her affairs in retirement, she decided that gift annuities were the answer. She had no family responsibilities; she was not interested in her principal; she did not want the trouble of managing an investment portfolio. She merely wanted an income for life, regardless of how long she lived. She learned that her church and the American Bible Society paid an annuity rate of 5.5 per cent at her age. Since annuities are usually paid twice a year, she bought six annuities and spread them out over the calendar year so that she received a check each month. Gift annuities are so calculated that they will provide at least 50 per cent of the residuum for the charity at the time of the death of the annuitant. Thus Miss Y was assured (1) that she would have an adequate income for life, and (2) that her favorite Christian charities would on the average receive at least half the face value of the annuities.

Annuities are often written on *two* lives, so that both husband and wife are protected. The two lives need not be in the same family nor do they need to be of the same generation (although the rate is based on both of the lives). For the widow of advanced years with little knowledge of business and with a desire to help a Christian cause, the gift annuity offers great advantages.

The life-income agreements This is another form of giving while living. Mr. and Mrs. J had an excellent farm in central Iowa worth $125,000. They had other securities totaling about $75,000. What were they going to do with the $200,000 now that they were retired and planning to move to Whittier, California, where they already owned a small home? After investigating several plans, Mr. J decided on the "life-income agreement." He turned over the farm and securities worth $200,000 to his denominational foundation, for which he received an agreement whereby the foundation would pay him the average yield which the foundation received from its investment portfolio. (In recent years this yield has been 4.9 per cent.) Thus he and Mrs. J could count on about $9,800 a year, which would be enough to take care of them. Then, when both were gone, the denomination would receive 100 per cent of the capital. Mr. and Mrs. J would be living off the income; the capital would not be invaded. To make this plan even more attractive, some foundations invest the money in a segregated portfolio of tax-free securities, and the income to the recipient is also tax-free. However, there is a significant tax benefit, even when the principal is not invested in non-taxable securities.

The life-income agreement requires a somewhat larger amount of resources than the gift annuity, but it has the great value that the entire sum goes to the designated charity.

Life insurance offers an effective channel of giving　Mr. R lost his wife about a year ago, at the age of seventy-one. They had married early and raised a large family, four boys and two girls. He had always carried a large amount of insurance. At first this was for the protection of his wife and children when they were small, then it was to make certain a good education for the children. One of the girls married during her junior year in college and did not get her degree, but the other five children graduated from college and are well established in their business and professional lives. Mr. R is never sure how many grandchildren he has, but the figure changes often. One of his sons became a professor of chemistry in a large Eastern university. Mr. R had a good pension, but little use for the $100,000 in paid-up life insurance which had done such a good job of protecting his wife and family over the years. Since all his children were well established, he considered what would be the best way to make use of it. He was especially grateful for the job that his denominational college had done for his youngsters. He talked the matter over with his pastor and decided to do something for the college. Through his insurance agent and the development officer of the college, he found that it was a simple matter to change the beneficiary from his wife, now deceased, to the college. Now he has the satisfaction of knowing that he is helping other young people to have the same advantages his own children had.

Life insurance giving can follow another pattern. Mr. S got through school in a hurry. In his senior year in college he was picked by a large corporation as an "officer candidate." He made it. Now, at the age of thirty-five, he is associate vice-president in charge of sales training, and he will go higher. He does not have much money saved, but he has a large income for a man in the mid-thirties. He is on the board of a denominational hospital. That is where his four children were born and where his wife underwent an emergency appendectomy a few months ago. The hospital has a plan for expansion for a generation or two ahead. Mr. S knows it will always need money. He would like to give now, but he simply doesn't have the funds to do it. From the denominational paper he learned about a new "life insurance plan." Through the board of the hospital any donor could take out an insurance policy making the hospital the beneficiary. The size of the premiums depended on the age of the donor and the amount of insurance the donor wished to give to the institution. At his age the premium was about $25 per $1,000. He felt he could give $50,000 in this way. The entire amount of the premium was tax deductible because the hospital was the beneficiary.

For the man under fifty, with a large income, giving through life insurance can be one of the best means of making a large capital gift.

Trusts are an excellent means of charitable giving The donor sets aside a definite sum of money, property, or securities, and provides that the income shall be used for a charitable purpose for a given length of time. The variations on the trust idea are legion, providing for many types of situations. Trust instruments must be drawn up by an attorney. The types and kinds of trusts are too numerous to mention here.

Cash is always an acceptable gift This may seem like a truism, but it needs to be said. The charitable institution always has immediate use of the money. The donor has an immediate tax deduction. The money does not go into the estate and, thus, is readily available.

General principles in a program of wills and special gifts should be noted:

1. The family lawyer should write the will and should be consulted by the client on all major decisions regarding the transfer of capital funds. The will should be reviewed annually.

2. The church should stay out of the operation of businesses. Mr. X has a thriving dry cleaning business in Ourtown. He wants the First Presbygational Church to own and operate it, and pay him a small annuity. This would mean poor public relations for the firm, unfair competition, and probably poor business management. A better answer would be for Mr. X to work out an annuity agreement with one of the Presbygational denominational boards, where it would accept the business on an annuity agreement basis, sell the business in accordance with normal business practice under existing conditions, and provide Mr. X with an annuity on the dollar value of the proceeds of the sale. The holding of an investment portfolio does not constitute operating a business.

3. Endowments and substantial amounts for ready application to programs should be channeled away from congregations and toward more broadly representative boards of the denomination.

4. Stewardship excludes the sale of indulgences. Since Simon Magus tried to buy religious powers from the Apostle Paul, the church has been tempted to sell religious favors for money. The church has always needed the money. Sometimes it has not been above taking money in return for an assured place in heaven. In the Protestant tradition there is no place for works-righteousness. Man is saved only by the grace of God. No amount of money,

service, good deeds, or anything else can buy salvation. On the other hand, the Christian who has discovered the grace of God and experienced the love of Christ in his heart should be a new man whose life reflects the love of God. The fruitage is because of the grace of God, not in order to win the grace of God. Much so-called Christian generosity is little more than buying the esteem of the congregation and the community. Stewardship leaders should ever set before the people the highest motivations for Christian giving—love, gratitude, obedience.

5. The congregation should engage in a continuous low-pressure wills and special gifts program. Every congregation by whatever name should have a stewardship committee. Attached to this should be a "Wills and Special Gifts Subcommittee," composed of representatives from the professions of law, banking, business, accountancy, insurance, and sales wherever possible. This committee should be informed on the needs of the world Christian community and should be alert to call to the attention of the congregation the opportunities in the world about them: scholarships in the church college; new equipment needs in the hospital; rapidly developing homes for the aging; inner city mission work; new mission opportunities in the developing nations abroad; the better training of ministers and missionaries. A certain community in Minnesota has been prosperous in recent years. A great many of its citizens own shares in the community's major industry, whose stock has split several times. Such people should be informed about the advantages of giving appreciated securities. A wills and special gifts program should be in quiet operation the year around.

6. Denominational helps for this program are available. During the last fifteen years nearly every denomination in North America has organized (or in some cases reorganized) a foundation or "special gifts department." (A list of these will be found in Appendix B.) A letter to your denominational office will bring information on how to

secure the filmstrip "Over the Wall," or the color film "God's Will Through Yours," or the black-and-white film "Treasures in Heaven."

7. Christian commitment is the basis of a wills and special gifts program. There is little use trying to get a person to give to the church or its agencies until that person has first faced the question of his own relationship to Jesus Christ. Some may give token amounts to the church because "it is good for the community," but in the last analysis people should give to the church and its world-wide program because they want every man and woman to have the same joy in Christ which they have known. Few donors would set themselves up as ideal Christians, but at the same time they should have some sense of urgency about the work of Christ's Church in the world. That urgency can take many forms. Christian higher education is one of the crisis areas in America today. Church colleges need money badly. Many are doing superb jobs on limited resources. There is no satisfaction greater than helping young people grow into the full use of their latent powers. A few years ago Mr. Harold Thomas of Canton, Ohio, died at the age of sixty-one. About ten years before his death Mr. Thomas, his wife, and his mother-in-law gave to several church colleges in Ohio more than two million dollars on the annuity plan. During the last ten years of his life Mr. Thomas was able to see the good that his money was doing and to feel that he was in part responsible for the added effectiveness of these Christian colleges. His death was premature by modern standards, yet he had already experienced the rich joys of Christian stewardship for more than a decade.

7

AUDIO-VISUAL TOOLS

Dr. Harry S. Myers, executive secretary of the United Stewardship Council for its entire history (1920-1950) and recording secretary of the Department of Stewardship and Benevolence of the National Council of Churches from 1951 until his death on November 24, 1963, was a pioneer in the use of films for missionary and stewardship education. He began the use of 3¼x4¼-inch slides in 1903. About 1948 most communions shifted over from slides to filmstrips. In 1947 Dr. Henry Endress of the United Lutheran Church began a notable series of stewardship motion pictures with the widely used *And Now I See*, the story of a man's discovery of the world-wide ministries of his congregation. The most popular film in the history of the National Council of Churches is *The Will of Augusta Nash*, the story of a young professor's reaction to a $100,000 legacy from his great-aunt which is accompanied by the condition that he become a tither. More than 1,200 prints are in circulation. The most widely acclaimed filmstrip is *Reason for Being*, the story of a grandfather explaining the meaning of stewardship to his ten-year-old grandson. Audio-visual tools are essential in a stewardship program.

Instruction, not entertainment The American public has been trained to expect entertainment when the lights are dimmed and the picture flashes on the screen. For fifty years the "movie" has been the most popular form of diversion and recreation. The use of projected visual aids for any other purpose requires a shift of understanding. For the most part, the pleasure of entertainment films is derived by securing audience identification with attractive people doing interesting and unusual things. The film helps people escape from boredom. Stewardship films also seek identification through the use of attractive, intelligent people, but the basic goal is instruction, not entertainment. Facing life, rather than escaping it, is the purpose.

Program integration   Motion pictures and filmstrips are produced to fill a specific program need. No film should ever be shown in church solely for entertainment purposes. The film may have this incidental value, but the purpose should be instruction, information, or discussion. Denominational stewardship programs usually list titles which meet specific needs. An inspirational, motivational motion picture such as *Split-Level Family* is useful at the church program supper when the work of the church for the coming year is to be discussed. The denominations make filmstrips available for the training of Every Member Visitors. The most widely used film of this type is *Go Forth in His Name*, now ten years old but still valuable. A good filmstrip for the Wills Emphasis Committee is *Over the Wall*. The best recent motion picture on will-making is *God's Will Through Yours*. Most church films are prepared to stimulate group discussion in the Church. This is not easy because it is hard to shake off the spell of the darkened room and the identification with the characters presented. Discussion is necessary, however, because the issues raised in the film must be applied to everyday life.

Mechanics must be checked   The success of visual aids depends first of all upon a smooth mechanical performance. This check list should be followed:

√ Preview the film several weeks or months before the actual show date to be sure that it fits the program purpose you have in mind.

√ Regularly maintain the mechanical equipment in good operating condition. Have extra projection and "exciter" bulbs handy.

√ Train responsible youth in the church on the operation, care and maintenance of the projector.

√ Use the largest screen consistent with the size of the auditorium and viewing distance. Most churches should have at least two screens. Fill the screen with the picture.

√ Preview the entire film about two hours before the showing and leave the equipment in place, if possible. Check the circuits to make sure that the projector will remain "live" when the house lights are dimmed.

√ Plan the meeting so that the showing is an integral part of the hour or hour-and-a-half program.

√ Do not rewind the film during the discussion period.

√ Ship the print to its next destination within two hours after use, if possible. (This is good stewardship.) Report to the producer on the pros and cons of viewer reaction. Report to the depository any damage or technical difficulty.

√ Store equipment in a safe place.

√ Keep in mind that filmstrips require practice because of the synchronization of sound and picture.

Nonprojected visual aids Films are a recent event in human history. Man has a fundamental urge to interpret his world by artistic representations of reality as he sees it. The fish was one of the earliest symbols of Christianity because the Greek word *ichthus* (fish) was an acrostic meaning "Jesus Christ God Saviour." A wide variety of visual tools is available. Every church has one or more bulletin boards. A 4x5-inch, neatly lettered card can carry impact. Posters do a job even for "hit-and-run" passersby. Flo-brush pencils make posters easy for all. Display panels (perhaps on glass separator screens) offer effective space. Miniature "stained glass" windows made from oiled paper can tell a story. Flannel boards can be easily constructed from almost any kind of cloth, reinforced with sandpaper for easy attachment to the other surface. Papier-mâché offers a third dimension. Exhibits of Bibles, missionary pictures, letters, or handcrafts increase interest. Pantomime with living figures presents excellent possibilities.

Drama Many churches today are equipped with adequate stages. A simple but significant skit can often be put together in a few hours. Serious drama is difficult but rewarding. A new book, *There Were Twelve*, by Robert Casemore, contains twelve stewardship plays ranging in length from fifteen minutes to one hour, and in cast from two persons to thirteen. It is available from the stewardship departments of the communions.

Resources Every church should have a copy of the *Audio-Visual Resource Guide* published every two years by the Department of Audio-Visual and Broadcast Education of the National Council of Churches. This guide provides descriptions of more than 3,750 titles and is available from the Office of Publication, National Council of Churches, 475 Riverside Drive, New York, N. Y. 10027.

Filmstrips Many people mistakenly think that a filmstrip is a "poor man's movie." Filmstrips are primarily for instruction, while motion pictures are more for inspiration. The still pictures which make up a filmstrip provide excellent educational opportunities. The filmstrip recording provides a full range of sound possibilities. Filmstrips usually sell for from $5 to $12 (less when subsidized) and, thus, congregations should be able to purchase prints. This permits their use on the exact date desired and reuse at any time thereafter. Most filmstrips are good for at least five years and, if properly handled, may be used several hundred times. The following list of filmstrips is based upon relevance and availability. There is some overlapping on specific program topics. For example, several filmstrips are on the theme of visitor training. All of these filmstrips are worthy of a place in the congregation's library. Contact your denominational stewardship office for filmstrips recommended and sold.

SOUND FILMSTRIPS

The Miracle of Warren Walker

The story of a carpenter who learns that his hard-earned money is part of himself. When he gives it to the church, he is, in effect, giving part of himself to carry on the work of the church in all parts of the world.

Over the Wall

A motivation filmstrip to help people see the writing of a will as an act of Christian stewardship. The turnover side of the record gives instructions to the wills committee in the congregation.

Reason for Being

A grandfather explains to his grandson, through the use of seeds, pictures of his own childhood, etc., the reason for man's being as growing toward and giving himself to God. The photography is outstanding and the narration is suitable for juniors through adults.

Seek Ye First

A young couple, who have just joined the church, receive a letter from a layman on the basic obligations of church membership based on the theme, "Seek ye first the Kingdom of God." Church membership is in worshiping God and sharing yourself, your Christian faith, and what you have with God and your fellow men.

A Tip or a Talent

For high school youth, this strip helps them to evaluate their giving to the church in comparison to their spending for other purposes.

The Users

Detailed instruction for the building of a family budget based on Christian values. For a session following showing of the motion picture *The Spenders*. Excellent for marriage counseling.

The Plan

Stewardship for youth of today. So many things to do, places to go; so little income and so many things desired! Excellent for junior and senior high groups. Useful throughout year because of emphasis on vocation.

EMC Visitor Training Kit

This kit contains two filmstrips, piggy-back: *Profile of a Steward* and *Day for Decision*. Also "A Baker's Dozen," 33-rpm recording. Twelve situations visitors might experience on a call. To be used as discussion starters in training sessions for visitors.

Missionary films which give a graphic report of the work of Christ in other parts of the world should be in every congregation's year-round program. An outstanding example is *Epistle From The Koreans*, produced by the United Presbyterian Church, U.S.A. The stewardship films listed below touch on many themes such as vocation, Christian higher education, and evangelism. Check their availability from your denominational stewardship office or film depository.

MOTION PICTURES

All for Him   B & W—30 minutes

Bill and Peggy Jackson, newlyweds, are looking over their household accounts in their small, partially furnished apartment when Peggy questions the size of the tithe for the church. Bill then tells her the story of his boss, Mr. Thompson, who based his entire business on the policy of giving one-tenth of his profits to the church in spite of criticism by his assistant. Mr. Thompson firmly believed that if you put God first, everything else will sort of fit together where it belongs. Peggy then agrees that rugs and curtains aren't the most important things right now.

All That I Have   B & W—65 minutes

Dr. Grayson, a noted surgeon, now retired, is in court facing charges brought by his nephews that he is mentally incompetent to manage his considerable wealth.

The evidence against Dr. Grayson, as well as his own story, is presented in the form of "flashbacks" to scenes in which he gave or decided to give money to others. He had given a thank-offering of $50,000 to his church.

Dr. Grayson's explanation convinces the court (as well as the audience) not only of his competence, but of his integrity as a Christian: he had become convinced of the need to use his money for God's purposes, as urged in his pastor's sermon on stewardship.

And Now I See   B & W—30 minutes

This is the story of a church official and his growth in Christian stewardship. When George Miller, a businessman with time and talents, is elected to the official board, he has little vision of the Lord's work and little understanding of Christian stewardship. He has always taken God's blessings for granted and never felt an inner drive to do God's work. Two years later he is a changed man. The film shows the experiences which have brought about his growth as a Christian and a churchman.

The Beginning   B & W—44 minutes

The Stryker family has an unusual experience in church. Father, mother, and son Chuck decide to tithe. Mrs. Stryker signs for the daughter Eunice, a nurse. Tells of family struggle to keep their pledges, the resulting contributions of each— Eunice plays the organ, Wilson Stryker and Chuck repair the church roof, and Mrs. Stryker finds the deeper meaning in stewardship when she visits a prospective church member, finds her ill, and then cleans her house and cares for her sick and crying child.

Beyond Our Own   B & W—30 minutes

Two brothers, Bob and Peter Rogers, stars on their college football team and popular with their friends, are headed for success when they leave school: Bob, as a doctor, Peter as an attorney.

But Bob, wanting something more out of life, becomes a medical missionary in China. Peter, a nominal church member, becomes so absorbed in his career that when his beloved only son is killed in an accident he lacks the spiritual stamina to carry on. Persuaded to visit Bob in China, he finds the real meaning of the Christian faith in the sacrificial life of Bob and the devoted Christian Chinese. Excellent for evangelism, worship, or motivation to support Christian missions.

Buyers' Choice   Color, B & W—29 minutes

The Bensons have been uprooted from their former home and forced to move half-way across the country to Mr. Benson's new job. They must move in thirty days from the house they are presently renting. They call a family council to decide whether to buy a new home now. The Bensons' daughter will soon be going to college. However, if Mrs. Benson goes to work and the family economizes they should be able to buy the new house. The family must deal with such questions as: Would the expensive home be the best investment in the long run? Is it wrong to want to live better?

The Candlemaker   Color—13 minutes

Sparkling, good-humored, reverent, animated film. Tommy helps make candles—and agrees to give his finest candle to light up Jesus' cross on the altar. But the boy plays with his pet mouse, Squeaky, and forgets to put in the candlewick. Out of this incident grows a fascinating story and lesson, delightful and thought-provoking for all.

Christian Stewardship   B & W—18 minutes

Carl Fisher finds himself in a situation that forces him to think through his own idea of stewardship. His compelling problem will guide your discussion group into self-examination of its own stewardship attitudes. Raises such questions as "What *does* Christian stewardship include?" "Is my giving only between me and my God, or are others involved, too?"

For Good or Evil   B & W—45 minutes

This is a dramatic film about the meaning of money, the Christian attitude toward it, and the Christian use of it. It concerns three close friends: Dr. Spencer, banker Harper, and farmer Sam Williams.

Dr. Spencer delivered Sam's first child, Fred, and he and Harper were godfathers at the baby's baptism. But through the years their interests diverged—from each other and from the church. Fred, now married, works in Harper's bank. Fred and his wife, enjoying social life, have no time for the church. Fred, needing money desperately, takes a sum from his cash drawer at the bank. Harper, on learning of this, is enraged and threatens jail.

The pastor, asked by Fred's father for help, persuades Dr. Spencer to help raise the money. Then in a dramatic scene in the bank vault, he confronts the banker, Fred's godfather, and convinces him that money must be used for God's glory, not for personal power.

The Gift   Color—21 minutes

The film opens with a condensed account of the life of Christ, expressing the core of Christian belief. After Christ's resurrection we see the growth of the Church, composed of members who, unlike Christ, were imperfect. The Church experienced temptation and inner division of personality and soul. In spite of its tensions, this procession of believers became the Church we know today.

Today the Christian is assailed and confused by contemporary attitudes which oppose Christ's teachings. Modern man is divided. He is tempted to soothe his own conscience by performing half-measures as he lives and works in the Church. The way out of this dilemma is to re-examine the task of the individual steward. Christ's total gift is our example and our salvation. Our faith leads to gratitude and a desire to become a Christian steward. Only the whole man, wholly united with God, can himself be whole. This reconciliation is the urgent task of the Church and of each member.

The film uses a technique known as animated painting. It is quite different from the ordinary concept of animation and is in a class by itself. This is a deeply moving film useful with seniors, older youth, and adults. With careful preparation and control it might be used with juniors as well. Should be shown twice.

God's Will Through Yours   Color, B & W—29 minutes

The story of Gale Atkins, a young widow whose father's will was hard to find and then was discovered to be undated and unsigned. Pastor Kirkwood helps a neighboring couple work out their desire to help the church.

The Hidden Heart   B & W—30 minutes

Stephen Ware and his wife Ellen are suddenly faced with the fact that their daughter Charlotte is living by values altogether different from the values they have outwardly adopted for themselves. Charlotte's rejection of a young man of high ideals, but modest income, presents the immediate cause for facing up to the direction life is taking in this family where comfort and security have become the determining forces.

Their son Phil has just returned from a church work camp where he has become an enthusiastic supporter of a medical missionary enterprise in India. In rapid succession a series of dramatic events emerge from the relationships of this family that cause Stephen and his wife to make a complete rededication of their lives to the higher values which all along they had recognized but could not quite accept for themselves.

Excellent to motivate youth and students toward Christian lifework.

Money for the Master   B & W—30 minutes

This is a story of striking contrast—a story of an elderly lady, her dollars, and her generous stewardship. The dramatic contrast of the charity of a dedicated woman of meager means and a wealthy couple who lack the satisfactions that result from a life of selflessness and devotion to Christ. The climax is reached when the wealthy couple are brought to realize that Christ expects them to contribute of their worldly possessions as the Lord has prospered them. Useful in presenting the stewardship of money.

Salt of the Earth   B & W—50 minutes

This is the story of a layman's experience in stewardship and evangelism. A miner who has never taken God seriously inadvertently causes a fellow miner to be seriously injured. The man changes his outlook and, through the local pastor and church, finds the meaning of Christian life stewardship.

Well-produced against authentic backgrounds, this film shows well the relation of faith in God to life situations. With explanation of the scene which shows communion being administered to injured men in the mine, the film may be shown to non-Lutheran groups. Its evangelistic emphasis makes it suitable for worship services, but it also may be used to inspire workers making stewardship or evangelistic calls.

Second Chance   B & W—70 minutes

Every community, every church, has in it many people like Ed and Emily Dean—a popular young couple who started off their married life as enthusiastic workers in the church and who, as their family grew and their income increased, had less and less time for the church and for each other.

When death threatened, Emily suddenly saw her life in true perspective and when, in rare good fortune, the threat vanished, she humbly and sincerely thanked God for her "second chance."

This unusually fine film, based on a story by Faith Baldwin, was produced by the Protestant Film Commission. By posing in vivid, highly dramatic form the question of what you would do if you had your life to live over again, it provides solid food for thought on what to do with your life now, and on your relationship to God as steward of all he has given you.

The Secret of the Gift   Color, B & W—28 minutes

This film takes us behind the scenes in the lives of several members of a large church, and we see the reasons for the way they give. For one person it is gratitude; for another it is the result of sensing the needs of others. Another realizes that giving money is only part of the larger stewardship of time and effort.

The Spenders   B & W—24 minutes

Designed to help families rethink their family budgets in the light of a Christian standard of values. An older brother, about thirty-five years old, and his family do well on a limited income.

The younger brother, about twenty-eight, and his wife do poorly with a much larger income. To be used with a definite program of Christian family money management.

Split-Level Family   Color, B & W—29 minutes

This is the true-to-life story of a rather typical middle-class American family. Nominally interested in the church, they are confronted with the contemporary dilemma of financing their dream home on a real budget. The parents come to sense the conflict of values involved in the outlay of time and money through the example of their teenage daughter, who realizes one day how little she is really giving to the church. The film points up the attitude changes, decisions, and the spirit of rededication experienced by an average church family.

Treasure at Bethany   B & W—33 minutes

The story of a graduate student's discovery that people are the real "treasure" in any church, by his work with a gang of fourteen and fifteen-year-old boys in a slum area church. The purpose of this half-hour drama is threefold: to convince American Protestants that each individual has a responsibility to support his church; that such support involves the giving of one's self as well as the giving of money; and that the church has a stewardship responsibility to the people in its community.

Treasures in Heaven   B & W—29 minutes

A lawyer tells three stories about why everyone needs a will as a part of Christian stewardship.

The Will of Augusta Nash   B & W—34 minutes

Donald Nash, a professor at a small private college, receives an unusual bequest from his late aunt, Augusta Nash. Her will provides that he shall receive $100,000 provided that he becomes a tither. As Professor Nash wrestles with the decision of whether to become a tither, the audience is led to see tithing not as a fixed or legalistic requirement, but as a responsible Christian response to God's grace in Christ.

A *Wonderful Life*   B & W—45 minutes

This story is built around the real life of one of those rare characters, lovable and thoroughly human, whose greatest satisfaction is to serve God and his fellow men through his church.

Henry Wood was not the sanctimonious type, but a real man among men. He was both the despair and joy of his family. They shuddered at the way he drove their old car, sometimes felt that his quiet gifts to charity were their sacrifices, that the time he gave to the church was their loss. But at his death they knew that in his life they had found the meaning of living— for Henry Wood was in all ways a conscientious steward of his time and of his small possessions. To know him was to realize that this was a man who knew God.

8

AN ANNOTATED BIBLIOGRAPHY

Voluntary giving as the basic pattern of church support in the modern era is largely a North American phenomenon. By 1833 tax support for churches had disappeared. Few theologians got around to writing a rationale for voluntary church support or for individual Christian stewardship. Horace Bushnell could have written such a book. The historical survey of stewardship in Luther Powell's *Money and the Church* shows the paucity of materials. Since 1946, with the renewed interest in theology, the number of stewardship books has increased.

Stewardship is closely linked with promotion. Much of the useful literature is of the leaflet and booklet variety, not easily adapted for bibliographic purposes. A serious study such as that of Dr. John Lankford of Wisconsin State College, River Falls, Wisconsin, author of *Protestant Stewardship and Benevolence, 1900-1940*, is at a disadvantage in getting at the best current materials of a specific historical period.

The following bibliography is based upon materials of the recent past (since 1900) which are available in good libraries.

A. Books and Pamphlets

1. *General Philanthropy*

Andrews, F. Emerson, and Walton, Ann D., ed., *The Foundation Directory*, 2nd ed. New York: Russell Sage Foundation, 1964. A listing of philanthropic foundations having assets of more than $10,000. A necessary tool for understanding philanthropy in America.

ANDREWS, FRANK M., A *Study of Company-Sponsored Foundations*. New York: Russell Sage Foundation, 1960. A growing aspect of American philanthropy examined by the son of F. Emerson Andrews.

CURTI, MERLE, *American Philanthropy Abroad*. New Brunswick, N. J.: Rutgers University Press, 1963. Excellent chapter on religious benevolence. Impossibly large subject makes book incomplete in spots.

FOSDICK, RAYMOND B., *Adventure in Giving: The Story of the General Education Board*. New York: Harper & Row, Publishers, Inc., 1962. Documentation on one of Rockefeller's great philanthropic projects.

LENSKI, GERHARD, *The Religious Factor, A Sociological Study of Religion's Impact on Politics, Economics, and Family Life*. New York: Doubleday & Co., Inc., 1961. A Detroit study which shows effect of economic status on religious groupings.

MARTS, ARNAUD C., *Philanthropy's Role in Civilization: Its Contribution to Human Freedom*. New York: Harper & Row, Publishers, Inc., 1953. Widely experienced fundraiser shares his rich philosophy of giving.

2. General Reference

NORDOFF, CHARLES, and HALL, JAMES NORMAN, *Pitcairn's Island* (part of *Bounty Trilogy*). Boston: Little, Brown & Co., 1940. 903 pp.

STRUNK, WILLIAM, JR., and WHITE, E. B., *The Elements of Style*. New York: The Macmillan Co., 1959. 71 pp.

3. History of Stewardship

BOYD, CATHERINE E., *Tithes and Parishes in Medieval Italy: The Historical Roots of a Modern Problem*. Published for the American Historical Association. Ithaca, N. Y.: Cornell University Press, 1952. 280 pp. An important study which shows the pitfalls of a legally enforceable tax for church support.

BREMNER, ROBERT H., *American Philanthropy*. Chicago: University Press, 1960. 213 pp. A popular history of giving with emphasis on large philanthropists. A sketchy treatment.

CALKINS, HARVEY R., *A Man and His Money*. New York: Methodist Book Concern, 1914. 367 pp. A key book in the history of American stewardship. Contains a history of giving, an analysis of stewardship in relation to institutions and to history.

CENTRAL BOARD OF FINANCE OF THE CHURCH OF ENGLAND, *The Christian Stewardship of Money*. Westminster, England: Office of Information of the Church of England, 1959. 96 pp. A sensational rediscovery of classical Christian stewardship in the Church of England is described and documented.

DAVIS, J. MERLE, *New Buildings on Old Foundations: A Handbook on Stabilizing the Younger Churches in Their Environment*. Studies in the World Mission of Christianity, No. V. New York: International Missionary Council, 1945. 320 pp. A study of financial practices of the younger churches, showing that unless a church develops genuine economic roots its entire structure is liable to collapse.

CONSTABLE, GILES, *Monastic Tithes*. New York: Cambridge University Press, 1964.

JORDAN, WILBUR K., *Philanthropy in England*. Vol. I, 1480-1660. New York: Russell Sage Foundation, 1959. 409 pp.

——, *Charities of London*. Vol. II, 1480-1660. New York: Russell Sage Foundation, 1960. 463 pp.

——, *The Charities of Rural England*. Vol. III, 1480-1660. New York: Russell Sage Foundation, 1961. 484 pp. Especially useful for study of development of American legal and philanthropic tradition.

McCONAUGHY, DAVID, *Money, the Acid Test*. New York: Missionary Education Movement of the United States and Canada, 1919. 193 pp. The single most influential book on stewardship in North America in the twentieth century. Until his death in 1946 McConaughy was the acknowledged leader of the American stewardship movement.

McConnell, Francis J., *Christian Materialism*. New York: Friendship Press, 1936. 167 pp. Out of the background of the Depression, Bishop McConnell discusses the getting, spending, and giving of money.

——, *Church Finance and Social Ethics*. New York: The Macmillan Co., 1920. 130 pp. Ethical issues in church endowment funds.

Powell, Luther P., *Money and the Church*. New York: Association Press, 1962. 356 pp. Excellent summary of the history of Christian giving.

Root, Edward T., *The Bible Economy of Plenty*. New York: Harper & Row, Publishers, Inc., 1939. 198 pp. A study of need for abundant production as proved from the Bible against a background of the depression of 1930-1940.

Salstrand, George A. E., *The Story of Stewardship in the U.S.A.* Grand Rapids, Mich.: Baker Book House, 1956. 169 pp. A history of stewardship. Weak on the United Stewardship Council (1920-1950) and entire period since 1940.

Tawney, R. H., *Religion and the Rise of Capitalism: A Historical Study*. Holland Lectures for 1922. Pelican Books. New York: Penguin Books, 1947. 280 pp. Classic tool for understanding the relationship of Christianity to property.

Weber, Max, *The Protestant Ethic and the Spirit of Capitalism*, trans. by Talcott Parsons. New York: Charles Scribner's Sons, 1958. 292 pp. A sociological classic relevant to the stewardship problem. The idea of "worldly asceticism" is closely linked to Protestant middle-class patterns of philanthropy.

Xenophon, *Memorabilia and Oeconomicus*, trans. by Edgar C. Marchant. Loeb Classical Library. Cambridge, Mass.: Harvard University Press, 1923. 531 pp. The first major book on stewardship, written about 400 B.C. Focus on farm management.

4. Methods of Stewardship

ACKERMAN, J. EMORY, and JOHNSON, F. ERNEST, *The Church as Employer, Money Raiser, and Investor*. New York: Harper and Brothers, 1959. 183 pp. This study shows that the church follows business ethics for the most part, with the notable exception that, lacking as much money, it does not offer as much financial security.

ANDREWS, F. EMERSON, *Attitudes Toward Giving*. New York: Russell Sage Foundation, 1953. 145 pp. This report of 91 "depth" interviews contains comparatively little information.

BRAMER, JOHN C., JR., *Efficient Church Business Management*. Philadelphia: Westminster Press, 1960. Excellent manual by laymen—theological teacher—businessmen.

BROOKS, LAWRENCE E., *Better Church Finance*. Anderson, Ind.: Warner Press, 1960. 64 pp. Emphasis on bookkeeping.

BYFIELD, RICHARD, and SHAW, JAMES, *Your Money and Your Church*. Garden City, N. Y.: Doubleday and Co., Inc., 1959. 238 pp. Heavy dependence on Wells' Organization techniques. Some theological insights for professional workers.

CASEMORE, ROBERT, *There Were Twelve*. New York: Department of Stewardship and Benevolence, National Council of Churches, 1964.

CASHMAN, ROBERT, *The Business Administration of a Church*. Chicago: Willett, Clark and Co., 1937. 163 pp. One chapter deals with church finance as seen from Chicago perspective in the mid-1930s.

——, *The Finances of a Church*. New York: Harper & Row, Publishers, Inc., 1949. 159 pp. A brief outline of the field based largely on one community church in Chicago.

COWLING, ELLIS, *Let's Think About Money*. New York: Abingdon Press, 1957. 95 pp. A down-to-earth discussion of the meaning of money from the standpoint of the individual Christian.

CROSSLAND, WELDON, *How to Increase Church Income*. New York: Abingdon Press, 1947. 159 pp. Heavy on gadgets.

DEXTER, HARRIET H., *Financing Faith*. St. Louis: Bethany Press, 1951. 127 pp. A discussion of the meaning of Christian stewardship for women.

DITZEN, LOWELL RUSSELL, *Handbook for the Church Secretary*. Englewood Cliffs, N. J.: Prentice-Hall, Inc., 1963. 229 pp.

GRAYBEAL, DAVID M., *The Christian Family and Its Money*. Woman's Division of Christian Service, Board of Missions, The Methodist Church. Literature Headquarters, 7820 Reading Road, Cincinnati 37, Ohio. 145 pp. Practical discussion of the economic problems of the family.

Handbook for *"The Christian Family and Money Management."* New York: Department of Stewardship and Benevolence, National Council of Churches, 1964. 15 pp.

HATCH, CLARENCE W., *Stewardship Enriches Life*. Anderson, Ind.: Warner Press, 1951. 107 pp. A typically American interpretation of stewardship and its implication for both individual and church life.

HERMANN, J. E., *The Chief Steward*. St. Louis: Lutheran Church—Missouri Synod, 1951. 115 pp. A handbook for pastors.

HOLCK, MANFRED, JR., *Accounting Methods for the Small Church*. Minneapolis: Augsburg Publishing House, 1961. 108 pp. An excellent manual.

HOLT, DAVID R., II, *Handbook of Church Finance*. New York: The Macmillan Co., 1960. 195 pp. Practical suggestions.

HYMN SOCIETY OF AMERICA, *Ten Stewardship Hymns*. New York: The Hymn Society of America, 1961.

JONES, G. CURTIS, *Handbook of Church Correspondence*. New York: The Macmillan Co., 1962. Good advice but largely based on a single large Middle Western church.

KEECH, WILLIAM J., *The Life I Owe*. Valley Forge: Judson Press, 1963. A manual for stewardship education for each age group, with focus on the family as the basic means.

KLIPHARDT, DONALD J., ed., *Audio-visual Resources Guide*, 6th ed. New York: National Council of the Churches of Christ in the U.S.A.

LINDHOLM, PAUL R., *Christian Stewardship and Church Finance*. New York: World Horizons, 1957. 330 pp. [Spanish edition: *Mayordomia Cristiana y Finanzas de la Iglesia.* Tomo I. Mexico, D. F.: Casa de Publicaciones "El Faro," 1958. 55 pp.] A practical day-by-day manual for teaching Christian stewardship in the younger churches. Designed to meet the needs of simple people in primitive economies.

McMULLEN, JOHN S., *Stewardship Unlimited.* Richmond, Va.: John Knox Press, 1961. 94 pp. Thirteen topics on practical stewardship for the layman.

McRAE, GLENN, *Teaching Christian Stewardship.* St. Louis: Bethany Press, 1954. 158 pp. Manual on stewardship education.

MILLER, RANDOLPH C., *Education for Christian Living,* 2nd ed. Englewood Cliffs, N. J.: Prentice-Hall, Inc., 1963. 462 pp.

OLSON, RAYMOND M., *Stewards Appointed.* Minneapolis: Augsburg Publishing House, 1958. 141 pp. A discussion of Christian stewardship based on Luther's Small Catechism —a splendid manual for confirmation classes.

PENDLETON, OTHNIEL A., JR., *New Techniques for Church Fund Raising.* New York: McGraw-Hill Book Co., 1955. 256 pp. An elaborate description of the famous "Eight-Point Plan" of the Every Member Canvass. Designed by Marts and Lundy professional fund-raising firm for the American Baptist Convention and widely adopted in the various communions of the United States and Canada.

RAY, GEORGE McNEILL, *Tall in His Presence.* New York: Seabury Press, 1961. 127 pp. Stresses responsibility as basis of stewardship. Legalistic interpretation of tithing as belonging to God.

SCHUMACHER, CURTIS R., *Adventures in Church Financing,* 3rd ed. New York: Board of Homeland Missions of the United Church of Christ, 1964. 74 pp. An excellent manual for a capital funds campaign in the congregation.

SLY, FLORENCE M., *Your Family and Christian Stewardship.* St. Louis: Bethany Press, 1958. 25 pp. A discussion of stewardship in the home.

WALLACE, HELEN K., *Stewardship for Today's Woman.* Westwood, N. J.: Fleming H. Revell Co., 1960. 94 pp. Woman in various roles: homemaker, mother, professional, widow, etc.

WARD, HILEY H., *Creative Giving*. New York: The Macmillan Co., 1958. 170 pp. An attempt to promote "spontaneity" as against "planned" giving of tithing.

5. Sermon Resources

APPLEGARTH, MARGARET T., *Twelve Baskets Full*. New York: Harper & Row, Publishers, Inc., 1957. 245 pp. A delightful mine of highly usable stories and meditations on the main theme of Christian stewardship.

CROWE, CHARLES M., *Stewardship Sermons*. New York: Abingdon Press, 1960. 141 pp. Excellent common sense and much present-day knowledge. Little basis in the gospel of Jesus Christ.

CUSHMAN, RALPH S., *The Message of Stewardship*, revised edition. New York: Abingdon-Cokesbury Press, 1946. 240 pp. Dated devotions from the 1940s.

KING, JULIUS, ed., *Successful Fund-Raising Sermons*. New York: Funk and Wagnalls, 1953. 274 pp. Excellent anthology.

KUNTZ, KENNETH, *Wooden Chalices*. St. Louis: The Bethany Press, 1963. 192 pp. Meditations and illustrations on stewardship. Excellent preaching materials.

ROBERTSON, A. T., *Word Pictures in the New Testament*. New York: R. R. Smith, Inc., 1930.

SMITH, ROY L., *Stewardship Studies*. New York: Abingdon Press, 1954. 251 pp. Brief comments on Scripture passages. Clever. Stimulating.

SOCKMAN, RALPH W., *The Fine Art of Using*. New York: Board of Missions and Church Extension of the Methodist Church, 1946. 125 pp. Excellent stewardship sermons by a master craftsman.

Twenty Stewardship Sermons. Minneapolis: Augsburg Publishing House, 1954.

6. Theology of Stewardship

AZARIAH, V. S., *Christian Giving*. New York: Association Press, 1939. New edition, 1955. 96 pp. An Anglican bishop of

India gives a classic interpretation of stewardship from the standpoint of Asia.

BRATTGARD, HELGE, *God's Stewards*. Minneapolis: Augsburg Publishing House, 1963. 248 pp. A Swedish theologian's interpretation of stewardship in America and Europe. Basically Biblical theology as interpreted by the Lutheran confessions. The best theological treatment of stewardship to date (1964).

BRUNNER, EMIL, *Christianity and Civilization*. New York: Charles Scribner's Sons, 1949. 167 pp. The chapter on "Wealth" is a good discussion of stewardship.

CONRAD, A. C., *The Divine Economy*. Grand Rapids, Mich.: Eerdmans Publishing Co., 1954. 169 pp. A Ph.D. thesis which discusses stewardship from the viewpoint of the Trinity. Stimulating, but author lacks the background of Oscar Cullman, whose writing treats much of the same theme.

FERRÉ, NELS F. S., *Making Religion Real*. New York: Harper & Row, Publishers, Inc., 1955. 157 pp. Chapter VII, "Making Religion Real Through Giving," useful.

——, *Strengthening the Spiritual Life*. New York: Harper & Row, Publishers, Inc., 1951. 63 pp. Excellent discussion of tithing and proportionate giving in Chapter IV.

FLETCHER, JOSEPH F., ed., *Christianity and Property*. Philadelphia: Westminster Press, 1947. 221 pp. A series of nine essays (eight by Anglicans and one by a Presbyterian) on the meaning of property in the Old Testament, New Testament, various periods of church history, and its special implications for the mid-twentieth century.

GORE, CHARLES, ed., *Property, Its Duties and Rights*. London: Macmillan & Co., Ltd., 1915. A series of essays by outstanding Anglican churchmen. Largely historical in treatment and covering the period to about 1910.

GRACE, FRANK, *The Concept of Property in Modern Christian Thought*. Urbana, Ill.: University of Illinois Press, 1953. 173 pp. A useful doctoral thesis.

GRANT, FREDERICK C., *The Economic Background of the Gospels*. London: Oxford University Press, 1926. 156 pp.

Stimulating treatment. Helps understand parables and problems of Jesus' time.

GULLIXSON, F. F., *Christus Emptor*. Minneapolis: Augsburg Publishing House, 1945. 81 pp. A discussion of stewardship in the light of various theories of the atonement.

KANTONEN, T. A., *A Theology for Christian Stewardship*. Philadelphia: Muhlenberg Press, 1956. 126 pp. German edition: *Lebendige Gemeinde: Theologie Der Haushalterschaft*. Stuttgart, Germany: Evangelisches Verlagswerk, 1959. 157 pp. Spanish edition: *El Porque de la Mayordomia*. Buenos Aires: La Aurora y la Reforma, 1961. Considered by many to be the best systematic theological treatment from North America on the doctrine of stewardship.

KAUFFMAN, MILO, *The Challenge of Christian Stewardship*. Scottdale, Penn.: Herald Press, 1955. 180 pp. A careful study by a Mennonite scholar.

KNUDSON, ALBERT C., *The Principles of Christian Ethics*. New York: Abingdon-Cokesbury Press, 1943. 314 pp. Some discussion of economic ethics involving stewardship.

LANKFORD, JOHN E., *"Protestant Stewardship and Benevolence: 1900-1941, a study in religious philanthropy."* Ph.D. thesis at the University of Wisconsin, 1962. Available on loan from Department of Stewardship and Benevolence, National Council of Churches, New York. A major contribution to understanding of Protestant giving. Conclusion is evident from the start. Protestants did not live up to their theology.

LUTHER, MARTIN, *Works*, Vol. I-VI. Philadelphia: Muhlenberg Press, 1943.

——, *"Treatise on Good Works"* (1520) Vol. I, trans. by W. A. Lambert, pp. 173-285.

——, *"Treatise Concerning the Blessed Sacrament,"* (1519) Vol. II, trans. by J. J. Schindel, pp. 7-31.

——, *"Treatise on Christian Liberty,"* (1520) Vol. II, trans. by W. A. Lambert, pp. 297-348.

——, *"Treatise on Usury,"* (1520) Vol. IV, trans. by Charles M. Jacobs, pp. 37-69.

——, "On Trading and Usury," (1524) Vol. IV, trans. by Charles M. Jacobs, pp. 9-36.
The word "stewardship" or *Haushaltershaff* appears infrequently in Luther's writing. The above selections are useful in studying the idea.

LUTHERAN WORLD FEDERATION, *Proceedings of the Third Assembly*, Minneapolis, Minnesota, August 15-25, 1957. Minneapolis: Augsburg Publishing House, 1957. 119 pp. (Pp. 65-75, "Free for Service in the World" by Edgar M. Carlson.) The Lutheran World Federation has been the only world confessional group interested in stewardship.

LUTTERMAN, KENNETH GORDON, "*Giving to Churches: A Sociological Study of the Contributions to Eight Catholic and Lutheran Churches*," a Ph.D. thesis, University of Wisconsin, 1962. Shows that there is not much difference between Catholic and Protestant giving in one Wisconsin city.

MCKAY, ARTHUR R., *Servants and Stewards*. Philadelphia: The Geneva Press, 1963. 76 pp. Problems of present-day (1963) stewardship.

MCLELLAND, JOSEPH C., *The Other Six Days*. Toronto: Burns and MacEachern, 1959. 121 pp. A discussion of the doctrines of stewardship and vocation from the standpoint of the Christian layman.

MORGAN, BRUCE, *Christians, The Church and Property*. Philadelphia: Westminster Press, 1963. 304 pp. Excellent chapters on stewardship.

MORRO, WILLIAM C., *Stewardship*. St. Louis: Bethany Press, 1932. 185 pp. A scholarly study of stewardship from Bible and church history. Strong statement against tithing and for proportionate giving.

RASMUSSEN, ALBERT T., *Christian Social Ethics*. Englewood Cliffs, N. J.: Prentice-Hall, Inc., 1956. 318 pp. Two good chapters on stewardship.

REUMANN, JOHN HENRY PAUL, "The Use of *Oikonomia* and Related Terms in Greek Sources to About 100 A.D. as a Background for Patristic Applications," a Ph.D. thesis at the University of Pennsylvania, 1957. Available on loan from the Department of Stewardship and Benevolence, National Council of Churches, New York. University Microfilm, Ann Arbor, Michigan. Best study of Greek language basis of idea of stewardship (*Oikonomia*).

ROLSTON, HOLMES, *Stewardship in the New Testament Church*. Revised edition. Richmond, Va.: John Knox Press, 1959. 160 pp. A discussion of the theology and practice of stewardship in the teachings of Paul.

STEWART, JAMES S., *Thine is the Kingdom*. New York: Charles Scribner's Sons, 1956. 74 pp. A theology of mission with many implications for a stewardship.

THOMAS, G. ERNEST, *To Whom Much is Given*. New York: Abingdon-Cokesbury Press, 1946. 160 pp. Discussion of stewardship as responsibility.

THOMAS, WINBURN T., ed., *Stewardship in Mission*. Englewood Cliffs, N. J.: Prentice-Hall, Inc., 1964. 128 pp.

THOMPSON, T. K., ed., *Christian Stewardship and Ecumenical Confrontation*. New York: Department of Stewardship and Benevolence, National Council of Churches, 1962. 101 pp. Proceedings of the World Council of Churches consultation on stewardship at Bossey in summer of 1961. Best summary of international situation regarding stewardship.

———, *Stewardship in Contemporary Theology*. New York: Association Press, 1960. 252 pp. Nine lectures by as many theologians and leaders of the stewardship movement. Deals with the development of the idea of stewardship through the Old Testament, New Testament, the theology of Paul, and present-day stewardship problems.

TRAVER, AMOS J., *Graceful Giving*. Philadelphia: Muhlenberg Press, 1946. 100 pp. A theological essay on the Christian's giving based on God's giving.

7. Tithing

HARRELL, COSTEN J., *Stewardship and the Tithe*. New York: Abingdon-Cokesbury Press, 1953. 61 pp. An enthusiastic and critical evaluation of tithing.

KEECH, WILLIAM J., *Why Tithe?* Valley Forge: Baptist Youth Fellowship, Judson Press, 1957. 25 pp. A scholarly statement favoring a non-legalistic approach.

LANSDELL, HENRY, *The Sacred Tenth.* London: Society for Promoting Christian Knowledge, 1906. 725 pp. Basic book on the history of the tithe.

SHEDD, CHARLIE W., *How to Develop a Tithing Church.* New York and Nashville: Abingdon Press, 1961. 123 pp. An excellent handbook. Tithing is interpreted broadly.

THOMAS, G. ERNEST, *Spiritual Life Through Tithing.* Nashville: Tidings, 1953. 104 pp. A strong commendation of tithing.

B. PERIODICAL ARTICLES

1. *History of Stewardship*

CARLSON, MARTIN E., "Stewardship: Christianity Lived Responsibly." *Centennial Essays,* Emmer Engberg, ed., Rock Island, Illinois: Augustana Press, 1960, pp. 247-67. Key article for understanding Augustana Lutheran stewardship tradition.

2. *Theology of Stewardship*

PIPER, OTTO, "That Strange Thing Money." *Theology Today,* Vol. 16 (July 1959), pp. 215-31.

STAGG, PAUL L., "An Interpretation of Christian Stewardship." *What is the Church.* Duke K. McCall, ed., Nashville: Broadman Press, 1958. 189 pp. An attempt to overcome legalism. Sharp Biblical insights.

C. UNPUBLISHED MATERIALS

1. *General Philanthropy*

NEBOLSINE, GEORGE, "Fiscal Aspects of Foundations and of Charitable Donations in European Countries." Available from the Foundation of European Culture, Singel 542, Amsterdam, The Netherlands. (Also available from Department of Stewardship and Benevolence, National Council of Churches, New York.) How laws do or do not encourage giving.

THOMPSON, T. K., "A Study of Philanthropy in Western Europe." 121-page manuscript available on loan from Russell Sage Foundation, 230 Park Avenue, New York. 1961-1962. (Also available on loan from Department of Stewardship and Benevolence, National Council of Churches, New York.) Secular and religious philanthropy against the background of the sensational economic recovery of Europe, 1950-1960.

2. History of Stewardship

THOMPSON, T. K., "Christian Stewardship in Western Europe: 1961-62." A study in mimeographed form, available from Department of Stewardship and Benevolence, National Council of Churches, New York. A brief summary of stewardship and church finance in eleven countries.

9

CAPITAL FUNDS
FOR THE CONGREGATION

About once every twenty-five years an established congregation faces the need for capital funds. With new congregations
the need of capital funds for the first twenty years is almost
overwhelming.

The need for building funds A short depression followed
World War I, but the prosperity of the period 1922-29 was
hardly reflected in the giving of the churches. A backlog of
building needs began to accumulate beginning in 1926. Almost
no church building took place during the depression of 1929-
40. War and postwar priorities stopped church construction
from 1940 to 1947. About 1950 the dam broke. Virtually every
congregation in the country built a new educational building,
sanctuary, chancel, parking lot, or parsonage. Part of this boom
was spearheaded by returning servicemen who filled the church
nurseries with children, the offering plates with money, and the
church boards with demands for more adequate equipment.
The war had accelerated the move from the country to the
city, and the suburbs were deluged with needs for new churches
or vastly enlarged existing ones. During the decade of the Fifties
church attendance, membership, and giving climbed rapidly.
(The Sixties, so far, represent something of a plateau.) Higher
standards of Christian education were required by better-edu-

cated young parents. Youth choirs, week day schools, and vacation schools made better use of church school rooms. The theological revival of 1930-60 increased the number of informal Bible study groups. While $10- or $12-billion dollars have been spent on church building since 1947, probably an equal amount needs to be invested to keep up with the population explosion. The bumper "baby crop" of 1946-49 will soon be entering the marriageable age and the population of the nation is expected to double in the next thirty years.

The development of professional fund-raising counsel Since the work of the pioneer, Charles S. Ward, the fund-raising profession has progressed to a point where a philanthropic organization in need of funds today will almost certainly retain professional counsel. Congregations before 1950 were slow to employ professional fund-raising counsel for several reasons: they thought they could raise as much money by themselves; they considered the funds raised to be "God's money" and therefore not to be spent for some "outside" organization; they were suspicious that some "expert" might trick them into giving more than they planned. During the last fifteen years congregations have done an almost complete "about face" on this matter. They now feel that fund-raising counsel is as necessary as architectural counsel.[1]

The development of denominational services Virtually all Protestant communions now have capital funds services. These denominational agencies are associated in the Committee on Capital Funds of the Department of Stewardship and Benevolence of the National Council of Churches. (See Appendix C for a list of these offices.) John Van Iderstine of the Lutheran Church in America Fund-Raising Service has suggested the following points in the consideration of professional fund-raising counsel:[2]

---

[1] For information regarding professional fund-raising organizations, write the American Association of Fund-Raising Counsel, 500 Fifth Avenue, New York, N. Y.

[2] Adapted from an article by John I. Van Iderstine, "So You Are Going to Raise Capital Funds!" *Stewardship Facts 1963-64.*

1. Check first on the professional services offered by your own denomination. (See Appendix A.) The advantages are: Christian stewardship will be a part of the program, and the services will be tailored to the tradition and needs of the denomination.

2. Choose the agency that will provide the best services for your congregation. Check references carefully.

3. Require resident direction.

4. Explore pre-campaign and follow-up services.

5. Demand a flat fee basis.

6. Secure information from the American Association of Fund-Raising Counsel mentioned above or from the Department of Stewardship and Benevolence of the National Council of Churches.

Steps in a typical campaign Perhaps the best book in the field of capital funds for the congregation is Curtis Schumacher's *Adventures in Church Financing.*[3] Schumacher, Van Iderstine, and other authorities are agreed that a capital funds campaign incorporates the following basic features:

1. Christian stewardship must be the basis of all church giving. This requires a study of the New Testament and a commitment to Jesus Christ.

2. Program needs dictate the design of the new facility.

3. Detailed information must reach every possible donor by a variety of media: letters, discussion, brochures, visits. Enthusiastic support of the plan is necessary from a substantial majority.

4. Professional architectural and fund-raising services will create confidence.

5. A follow-up program of interpretation and contact will ready the congregation for the next phase of development.

---

[3] Available from the Church Finance Advisory Service of the United Church Board for Homeland Ministries, 287 Park Avenue South, New York, N. Y. 10010 ($1.65) or Department of Church Architecture, Division of Home Missions, National Council of Churches, 475 Riverside Drive, New York, N. Y. 10027.

Checkpoints in a building program So many churches have carried out building programs in the last dozen years that other congregations have asked themselves, "Don't we need to build, too? Everybody else is doing it." Some searching questions need to be asked:

1. Local needs in the light of world Christian needs. Stewardship applies to congregations as well as to individuals. A new organ in Middleville might cost as much as a hospital in Africa. Full carpeting for the new educational building might build a sanctuary in India.

2. One-hour-a-week use. Multiple-use rooms overcome the possible criticism of expensive little-used facilities.

3. Long-range planning. The success of the campaign will depend on the number of people committed to the project. Adequate information and discussion require a year.

4. Training visitors. The most important by-product of the campaign will be a large number of workers who understand the work of the church and who are committed to its success.

5. Freedom for the architect. Program specifications should be precisely worked out and handed to the architect along with a suggested dollar amount for the project. Frequent consultations in the early stages of the plans will help. It should be remembered, however, that the architect is an artist and should have freedom to develop ideas.

6. Short cuts. The capital funds campaign is a complicated affair in which people can easily be alienated by seemingly unimportant details. The best answer is to get a good professional and follow his directions enthusiastically.

7. Christian joy. Two of the thrilling stories in the Old Testament are those of the collections for the Tabernacle and the building of the Temple. The privilege of building a house to God was denied to David. Building a house of worship is one of the great acts of Christian stewardship.

Capital funds outside the congregation Your congregation is a member of a national fellowship of churches. Just as the congregation from time to time has needs for capital funds, so too the state and national agencies of your denomination need them. This is because the church is people, and the population of North America and the world is growing rapidly. The post-war baby boom is now engulfing the church-related colleges. The demand for better hospital care has put pressure on church hospitals. Suburbia is clamoring for more new churches. Overseas the opportunities are even more impressive. The new nations of Africa have an immediate need for trained Christian leaders. The industrial cities of India need new churches as well as new steel mills. When these state and national denominational capital funds programs reach the congregational level, the local church should respond in a spirit of Christian stewardship. The congregation is a part of a world-wide Christian fellowship. The sharing of men and money is mutually enriching.[4] These denominational capital funds campaigns are carefully worked out, and the best pattern is for the congregation to enthusiastically carry out the plans which have been democratically reached through the representative government of the communion.

[4] See *Stewardship in Mission*, edited by Winburn T. Thomas (Englewood Cliffs, N. J.: Prentice-Hall, Inc., 1964).

10

STEWARDSHIP AND PREACHING

Dr. John Herrmann, Director of Stewardship for the Lutheran Church—Missouri Synod, in his book for pastors, *The Chief Steward*, maintains that the example of the pastor in giving, prayer, Bible study, and the use of time and money is the key to stewardship in the congregation. The pastor's life and home is open for all to see. Good preaching must be matched by good living. The same is true for all Christians: their lives should bear witness to their faith.

Preaching has become difficult in the twentieth century. Radio, movies, television, and recordings hurl millions of words at the listener every week. Newspapers and magazines add to this barrage. Unfortunately, the average preacher compares rather poorly with a good TV commentator. With a rapidly improving educational level among his hearers, the preacher must "sell" his ideas rather than quote authoritative sources.

In one respect the mid-twentieth century is better for preaching. People want action. They are not content merely to "believe" or give assent to sermons or traditions of the past. They want help in living. The goal of preaching is "faith-in-action" and "action-in-faith." At this point, stewardship is much more understandable than many of the doctrines of the faith: it is the Christian Gospel stated in economic terms. The stewardship ideal is not easier to follow, but it is understandable.

Bible study The pastor might well begin his study of the preaching program of the congregation with an examination of how his parishioners are growing in the knowledge of the Scriptures. For several years church life in Europe and North America has been characterized by small informal Bible study groups. Usually the groups meet in homes. Frequently a trained layman is in charge under the direction of the pastor. The purpose is the study of the Scriptures for guidance in practical living. Auxiliary guides, like Barclay's commentaries or the layman theological series of John Knox Press or the "Fortress" series of Muhlenberg Press, are often used. After a study of a passage the question always arises: "How does this help in the decisions I have to make?" The use of modern translations, such as those by J. B. Phillips and the New English Bible, help make the meaning vivid. A congregation ought to have at least 10 per cent of its adult membership engaged in continuous Bible study of this or some similar type.

Preaching as a part of Christian education In spite of the growth of Bible classes in the last dozen years, the average adult member of the congregation still has little contact with Bible study except through the sermon. This puts an even heavier responsibility on the pastor in regard to expository preaching. The same is true of the entire Christian education process. Most adult members of the church do not attend church school classes. The sermon and the worship service become their sole opportunity for education. The pastor will greatly benefit from his study of the books of Lewis Sherrill, Randolph C. Miller, and James Smart in respect to utilizing sound principles of Christian education in the preparation of sermons.

Preaching as a part of the experience of worship Many Protestants have been inclined to view the sermon as the "heart" of the worship service. Other elements in the order of service have been viewed as "opening exercises." Actually, worship is a dialogue-confrontation (to use words that are "necessary" in theological circles). The initiative comes from God making man restless until he finds rest in God. "Worship" literally is "worth-ship"—ascribing supreme worth to the "Supremely Worthful." After the pronouncement of forgiveness and the preaching of the Word, the worshippers respond by committing their lives to service in Christ's kingdom. This is symbolized in prayers, offerings, and in going out into the world. The offering of money should not be called a "sacrifice." It is rather the substantive symbol of the worshipper's self-giving. Christ alone is the perfect and final Sacrifice. Nothing that the Christian ever does should be put in the same context. Dom Gregory Dix's *The Shape of the Liturgy* provides helpful direction on this point. The Church of England has a Commission on Liturgy at work, and it will be interesting to see if they come up with a new recommendation regarding the place of the offering in the service. Some Protestants view the sermon as an offering in which the worshippers offer their hearts in faith to a hearing of the Word. In the moment the Word is faithfully preached and accepted, God is there.

Preaching as a channel of the Holy Spirit Stewardship is the ordering of the whole of life in accordance with the will of God revealed in Jesus Christ. The Holy Spirit is manifestly at work in scriptural exposition that is Christ-centered in emphasis and redemptive in purpose. A pastor can prepare the form and content of the sermon. But no sermon becomes the Word of God until the Holy Spirit becomes the activating agent in the heart of the Spirit-filled hearer. Belief comes mainly by the hearing of the Word. Belief is the precursor of action. The failure to live by one's faith is just that—failure. The church-going Christian cannot abandon the Holy Spirit on the church steps from one Sabbath to the next. God's Holy Spirit is ever present to inspire and to give grace-gifts to all believers humble enough to depend on Him and willing to be used as channels of Divine love.

Resources for preaching on stewardship The best "stewardship" message is the life of the pastor himself. The best sermon on stewardship is the Gospel itself: "God so loved . . . that He gave . . ." Nothing makes a man a steward more rapidly or more completely than to stand at the foot of the Cross and hear: "He that spared not His Own Son, but delivered Him up for us all, how shall He not freely with Him give us all things" (Romans 8:32).

Specific sermons on stewardship are necessary, however, and the following suggestions may be found useful.

The Bible is the best source for ideas and illustrations. It is useful to go through the Bible and mark each passage that deals with the three major principles of stewardship: God's ownership, man's creative servantship, and the final accounting. Since stewardship deals with the everyday life of housekeeping and home economics, almost every page will yield one or two markings. A list of possible sermon themes will be found in Appendix D.

Bible tools will yield rich fruit: a topical concordance, the new RSV Concordance, the new commentaries and Bible dictionaries, Rudolf Kittel's *Wörterbuch* in both German and English, Alan Richardson's *Theological Wordbook of the Bible*, and A. T. Robertson's *Word Pictures in the New Testament*.

Theological books often have direct values in stewardship preaching. Oscar Cullman's writings make much use of the *oikonomia* concept. Frederick C. Grant has maintained a lifelong interest in the economic questions of the Bible. Nels Ferré writes on the stewardship theme frequently. The best theological book on stewardship from Europe is Helge Brattgard's *God's Stewards*.

Stewardship illustrations frequently are difficult to find. Some preachers avoid using books of illustrations because they lack the personal flavor. Yet, ministers must be guarded in their use of illustrations from their own pastoral experience lest they "betray the confessional." Church history is an excellent source of illustrations, even though most historians have neglected the economic factors in the development of Christianity. The Reformation should have taught them otherwise.

Stewardship hymns are few. Most hymnals contain a section on "stewardship" or the "offering" or "consecration," but the well-known hymns are overworked, if not worn out. In 1960 the Hymn Society of America conducted a Stewardship Hymn Project, with 436 entries, the 10 best of which are printed in Appendix E.

Preaching on Every Member Visit or Stewardship Sunday
The message on the Sunday that pledges are made during the home visitation should be a Gospel sermon: what God has done in Jesus Christ. This sermon should make clear the great centralities of the Christian faith: God's love expressed in His giving of Jesus Christ, man's redemption through Christ's self-giving, God's call to sinful men to become fellow workers with Him in the saving of mankind, the church as the instrument of God for service in the world. The challenge to world-wide Christian work creates a favorable atmosphere for the visit. The commissioning of the visitors offers a special opportunity for a great call to dedication. The whole service on Stewardship Sunday should move in conviction of gratitude that God calls and uses men to do His work.

11

THE PRINTED WORD

The Protestant Reformation would probably not have been possible without the printing press. As long as the Latin Bible was chained to the scholar's desk, there was little chance that the common people could read the Word. The publishing world is indebted to the Christian Church for teaching the art of bookbinding, translation, manuscript illumination, and efficient distribution. History abounds with stories of how the Bible alone, as a printed book, without preacher or missionary, was responsible for the conversion of whole communities. *Pitcairn's Island* by Charles Nordoff and James N. Hall is one of the best stories of this kind.

Alert church officers will use all the literary resources at their command to further the cause of Christian stewardship.

Personal letter What is the most influential letter in history? This might be a matter of opinion, but certainly Paul's letter to the Romans stands near the top. Nearly every letter asks someone to do something. That "something" may be done to the glory of God. Dr. G. Curtis Jones has recently written an excellent "letter" on letter writing, *Handbook of Church Correspondence*.

Form letter Today's "organization" society requires many notices to many groups. Clear, action-producing letters are difficult to write. William Strunk and E. B. White's little book, *The Elements of Style*, has some concrete suggestions.

Sunday bulletin Virtually every congregation prepares mimeographed or printed bulletins for Sunday distribution. Occasionally there might be a paragraph on the world mission of the church, or the significant events of the week or month in the light of the Christian mission in those lands. A monthly report on monies received and expended keeps up interest the year around. Stencil inserts add variety to the format.

Local church paper Most congregations have a monthly newsletter which gives personal items, especially births, marriages, illnesses, and deaths. From time to time a missionary letter should be included. News of dedicated workers in the wider life of the church helps local church members identify with leaders in the church-at-large. Helpful suggestions for the editing of such a paper are found in Lowell R. Ditzen's *Handbook for Church Secretaries.*

Leaflet sources Most denominations prepare and make available stewardship leaflets without charge. These may be used effectively by inserting in parish letters, Sunday bulletins, or pew racks. The purpose of each such promotional leaflet should be clearly understood by the person assuming responsibility for its distribution within the local church.

Literature rack Every congregation should have a literature rack in the most accessible part of the church. Often this is in the parish hall rather than the vestibule of the sanctuary. It should be restocked every two weeks and straightened up every week. A clear-cut policy on use is needed lest the rack become an untidy depository for insignificant literature. An excellent addition to such a rack may be the "Reflection Book" series produced by Association Press. These inexpensive, hundred-page paperbacks cover titles of timely importance to the Christian.

Church library The great increase in the number of religious paperbacks has been a blessing to the church library. Many people are willing to donate or lend these low-cost books. Every congregation ought to have a library room or "library table" open at least two or three hours every Sunday. Public libraries are frequently willing to lend books to church libraries on a co-operative basis. Often a church's expression of interest will justify the purchase of a book by the public library. Friendship Press books are especially suitable for stewardship and missionary education.

Denominational stewardship materials Most communions send out two or three stewardship and promotion packets a year. Usually a letter or instruction sheet accompanies the packets. Speed and accuracy in preparing the order should be matched with the effective use of the materials once they are received.

Denominational magazine Each communion has a journal which informs its members of news in the life of the denomination and in the wider church world. Attractive rates are available for intensive coverage of the parish. Some congregations have provided in their budgets for free subscriptions and mailing to all families in the church. Subscriptions alone are not enough; occasional references to significant items in the paper from the pulpit and in church group meetings will increase intelligent use of the church journal.

Bulletin boards Every church ought to have at least two bulletin boards, one in the narthex and one near the door of the educational building. Announcements should be removed promptly when they are no longer relevant. Few, if any, notices should be allowed to stay more than a month. Only the person officially delegated should be allowed to place items on the boards. Homemade posters are effective. A poster-maker's guild might be organized and trained. Third-dimension displays win special attention.

The printed word gives wings to the Word.

EPILOGUE

This *Handbook of Stewardship Procedures* has dealt largely with the techniques by which a pastor and the stewardship committee of the congregation can effectively reach the members of the church. Stewardship will be most meaningful when Christian people bear daily witness by:

Loving all those who need love;

Sharing time and home and money with those who look for help;

Giving a worthy proportion of income every Sunday in worship;

Having a discretionary fund for all good causes;

Being sensitive to unexpressed hopes;

Paying one's bills promptly;

Expressing appreciation for services rendered;

Giving thanks to God and to the person God used to help;

Including among one's friends members of other races;

Helping all God's children get housing, jobs, education;

Enjoying God's gifts with exuberance: children, mountains, water;

Forgiving those who wrong us a little . . . and a lot;

Rejoicing in the victories of others which we would have liked to have won;

Knowing that beyond the Cross is the Resurrection.

Appendix A

United States

ADVENT CHRISTIAN CHURCH	917 Hardin Street, Aurora, Illinois
AMERICAN BAPTIST CONVENTION	Valley Forge, Pennsylvania 19481
BAPTIST GENERAL CONFERENCE	5750 North Ashland Avenue, Chicago 26, Illinois
NATIONAL BAPTIST CONVENTION, U.S.A.	2568 East 38th Street, Cleveland 15, Ohio
SOUTHERN BAPTIST CONVENTION	460 James Robertson Parkway, Nashville, Tennessee 37219
THE BRETHREN CHURCH	524 College Avenue, Ashland, Ohio
CHURCH OF THE BRETHREN	1451 Dundee Avenue, Elgin, Illinois 60120
CHURCH OF GOD (ANDERSON, IND.)	P.O. Box 2420, Anderson, Indiana
CHURCHES OF GOD IN N. AMERICA	Box 2103, Harrisburg, Pennsylvania 17105
CHURCH OF THE NAZARENE	6401 The Paseo, Kansas City, Missouri 64131
CHURCH OF THE NEW JERUSALEM	2504 128th Avenue, SE, Bellevue, Washington, D.C.
DISCIPLES OF CHRIST	222 South Downey Avenue, Indianapolis, Indiana
PROTESTANT EPISCOPAL CHURCH	815 Second Avenue, New York, New York 10017
EVANGELICAL CONGREGATIONAL CHURCH	750 North Second Street, Reading, Pennsylvania

EVANGELICAL COVENANT CHURCH OF AMERICA	5101 North Francisco Avenue, Chicago, Illinois
EVANGELICAL UNITED BRETHREN CHURCH	601 West Riverview Avenue, Dayton, Ohio
FIVE YEARS MEETING OF FRIENDS	101 Quaker Hill Drive, Richmond, Indiana
GREEK ORTHODOX ARCHDIOCESE OF N. AND S. AMERICA	319 East 74th Street, New York, New York 10021
THE AMERICAN LUTHERAN CHURCH	422 South Fifth Street, Minneapolis 15, Minnesota
LUTHERAN CHURCH IN AMERICA	231 Madison Avenue, New York, New York 10016
THE LUTHERAN CHURCH— MISSOURI SYNOD	210 North Broadway, St. Louis 2, Missouri
THE MENNONITE CHURCH	Mennonite Building, Scottdale, Pennsylvania
MENNONITE CHURCH, GENERAL CONFERENCE	722 Main Street, Newton, Kansas
AFRICAN METHODIST EPISCOPAL CHURCH	280 Hernando Street, Memphis, Tennessee
THE METHODIST CHURCH	1200 Davis Street, Evanston, Illinois
CUMBERLAND PRESBYTERIAN CHURCH	Box 5535, Memphis 4, Tennessee
PRESBYTERIAN CHURCH IN THE U.S.	341-C Ponce de Leon Avenue, N.E. Atlanta, Georgia
UNITED PRESBYTERIAN CHURCH, U.S.A.	475 Riverside Drive, New York, New York 10027
REFORMED CHURCH IN AMERICA	475 Riverside Drive, New York, New York 10027
SEVENTH-DAY ADVENTIST	6840 Eastern Avenue, NW, Washington 12, D. C.
UNITED CHURCH OF CHRIST	1505 Race Street, Philadelphia 2, Pennsylvania

Canada

ANGLICAN CHURCH OF CANADA	600 Jarvis Street, Toronto 5, Ontario, Canada
ATLANTIC UNITED BAPTIST CONVENTION	Box 1053, St. John, New Brunswick, Canada

BAPTIST CONVENTION OF ONTARIO AND QUEBEC	190 St. George Street, Toronto 5, Ontario, Canada
BAPTIST UNION OF WESTERN CANADA	9918 105th Street, Edmonton, Alberta, Canada
PRESBYTERIAN CHURCH IN CANADA	63 St. George Street, Toronto 5, Ontario, Canada
UNITED CHURCH OF CANADA	85 St. Clair Avenue East, Toronto, Ontario, Canada

Appendix B

Rev. James Austin, Director
Endowment & Capital Giving Promotion
Southern Baptist Convention
127 Ninth Avenue North
Nashville 3, Tennessee

Dr. Eugene R. Bertermann, Executive Director
Lutheran Church—Missouri Synod Foundation
210 North Broadway
St. Louis 2, Missouri

Mr. Ashby E. Bladen, Executive Director
Commission on Development
United Church of Christ
287 Park Avenue South
New York, N. Y. 10010

Mr. W. Nelson Bump, Executive Vice-President
Episcopal Church Foundation
815 Second Avenue
New York, N. Y. 10017

Dr. Paul V. Church, Executive Secretary
Evangelical United Brethren Church
General Council of Administration
601 West Riverview Avenue
Dayton 6, Ohio

Mr. A. Walton Litz, Acting Executive Director
The Presbyterian Foundation, Inc. (U.S.)
Wachovia Bank Building
Charlotte 2, North Carolina

Dr. Jonathan Gassett, Field Secretary
Wills, Annuities and Special Gifts
Church of the Nazarene

6401 The Paseo
Kansas City 31, Missouri

Dr. Don E. Hall
United Presbyterian Foundation
475 Riverside Drive
New York, N. Y. 10027

Rev. Roland K. Huff, Secretary
General Administration, Unified Promotion
Disciples of Christ
Box 19036
Indianapolis 19, Indiana

Mr. Alf W. Jorgenson, Field Counselor
The American Lutheran Church Foundation
422 South Fifth Street
Minneapolis 15, Minnesota

Dr. J. Homer Magee, Associate Secretary
Council of World Service and Finance
The Methodist Church
1200 Davis Street
Evanston, Illinois

Rev. George Morrison, Secretary
Board of Finance
United Church of Canada
85 St. Clair Avenue, East
Toronto 7, Ontario
Canada

Dr. Chester A. Myrom, Executive Director
Lutheran Church in America Foundation
231 Madison Avenue
New York, N. Y. 10016

Mr. Harl L. Russell
Director of Special Gifts
Church of the Brethren
1451 Dundee Avenue
Elgin, Illinois

Rev. David Stanfield, Secretary
Stewardship and Finance
Five Years Meeting of Friends
101 Quaker Hill Drive
Richmond, Indiana

Rev. Howard G. Teusink, Executive Secretary
Stewardship Council
Reformed Church in America
475 Riverside Drive
New York, N. Y. 10027

Mr. Eugene L. Warren, Executive Secretary
Board of Finance
Cumberland Presbyterian Church
1978 Union Avenue
Memphis 4, Tennessee

Rev. Robert L. Weaver, Associate Director
World Mission Campaign
American Baptist Convention
Valley Forge, Pennsylvania

Rev. Charles V. Weber, Executive Secretary
The Executive Council
Church of God (Anderson, Indiana)
Box 2420
Anderson, Indiana

Appendix C

Division of Church Extension
American Baptist Convention
Valley Forge, Pennsylvania

Church Building Campaigns
Church of God (Anderson)
Anderson, Indiana

Division of Church Extension
Church of the Nazarene
6401 The Paseo
Kansas City 10, Missouri

Promotion of Operational and Capital Budgets
Disciples of Christ
110 South Downey Street
Indianapolis 7, Indiana

Department of Stewardship
The American Lutheran Church
422 South Fifth Street
Minneapolis 15, Minnesota

LLM Fund-Raising Service
Lutheran Church in America
231 Madison Avenue
New York, N. Y. 10016

Department of Finance and Field Service
Division of National Missions
The Methodist Church
1701 Arch Street
Philadelphia 3, Pennsylvania

Church Building Campaign Department
United Presbyterian Church, U.S.A.

475 Riverside Drive
New York, N. Y. 10027

Church Finance Advisory Service
United Church of Christ
287 Park Avenue South
New York, N. Y. 10010

Department of Information and Stewardship
Anglican Church of Canada
600 Jarvis Street
Toronto 5, Ontario
Canada

Capital Funds Service
United Church of Canada
85 St. Clair Avenue East
Toronto 7, Ontario
Canada

Appendix D

Every pastor will want to develop a careful exegesis as the basis of his stewardship sermon. The following topics and scripture texts are suggested to give the pastor a quick survey of some possible themes. "Stewardship" is only one facet of the Gospel and quickly shades off into missions, evangelism, education, and many other concerns of the faith.

1. Fruits of the Field and Flock	Genesis 4:2
2. The Willing Heart	Exodus 25:1
3. The Tithe Is the Lord's	Leviticus 27:30
4. The Source of Wealth	Deuteronomy 8:18
5. Giving Out of Blessing	Deuteronomy 16:17
6. Choose Life: Love God	Deuteronomy 30:19
7. The Cost of the Offering	2 Samuel 24:24
8. God's Unfailing Pantry	1 Kings 17:14
9. Worship Through Offerings	1 Chronicles 16:27
10. Fruit in Season	Psalms 1:31
11. Sacrifices and Faith	Psalms 4:5
12. Goodness in Creation	Psalms 16:6
13. God's Prepared Table	Psalms 24:5
14. Who Owns What	Psalms 24:1
15. Stewards of Truth	Psalms 24:4
16. The Prior Owner	Psalms 50:10
17. A Sacrifice of Thanksgiving	Psalms 50:14
18. The Fearful Offering	Psalms 96:8
19. The Creator-Owner	Psalms 100:3
20. How to Thank God	Psalms 116:12-14
21. Wooden Idols	Isaiah 44:17
22. Unaccepted Sacrifices	Amos 4:46
23. Gifts for the King	Matthew 2:11
24. No Bread From Stones	Matthew 4:4
25. The Price of Power	Matthew 4:9
26. Man's Works and God's Glory	Matthew 5:16

113. A Sound Body
114. Working and Eating
115. The Bishop as House Manager
116. Deacons as Housekeepers
117. Example of Youth
118. Family Stewardship
119. The Love of Money
120. Christ, Guardian of Entrustments
121. Luke, Physician to the Apostle
122. Bishop as Steward
123. The Return of the Runaway Slave
124. Our Debt to Heroes of the Faith
125. The Origin of Gifts
126. The Fruits of Faith
127. Rotted Gold
128. God's Variety of Gifts
129. World's Hatred of the Loving Nonconformist
130. Givers Are Likest God
131. Keeping Faith With What We Have Received

1 Thessalonians 5:23
2 Thessalonians 3:11
1 Timothy 3:1-5
1 Timothy 3:8-13
1 Timothy 4:11,12
1 Timothy 5:8
1 Timothy 6:10
2 Timothy 1:14
2 Timothy 4:11
Titus 1:7
Philemon 18
Hebrews 11:32-40
James 1:17
James 2:17
James 5:1-6
1 Peter 4:10

1 John 4:11-18
1 John 4:7-21

Revelation 3:3

Appendix E

The following 10 hymns[1] were selected from a collection of 436 texts submitted in 1960 in response to an invitation submitted by the Department of Stewardship and Benevolence of the National Council of Churches in the U.S.A. and the Hymn Society of America for new hymn texts on stewardship.

In the initial instruction, it was designated that the hymns be written in the well-known meters traditionally found in standard church hymnals. The tunes suggested are largely those recommended by the authors. In most instances, more than one tune is indicated so as to provide the divergence of use in the various groups which will sing these tunes. The sequence is arranged alphabetically by authors.

---

[1] Ten New Stewardship Hymns, copyright 1961 by The Hymn Society of America; used by permission. Copies of the booklet containing these hymns are available from The Hymn Society of America, The Interchurch Center, 475 Riverside Drive, New York, N. Y. 10027 (prices available on request).

GIVE TO THE LORD AS HE HAS BLESSED THEE

9.8.9.8.8.8.
Tune: *Neumark.*(*Wer nur den lieben Gott*)
As arranged in the 1958 Hymnal of the Lutheran Church
in America.
(Some other hymnals have a different rhythm)

1. Give to the Lord, as he has blessed thee.
   Even when he seems far away,
   Know that his love has e'er possessed thee,
   Shelters and feeds thee every day.
   Heaven and earth are God's alone:
   Wilt thou hold back from him his own?

2. Give to the Lord, as he has blessed thee,
   Kept thee and guided from thy birth;
   Look to the day when death will wrest thee
   From all thy treasures here on earth.
   God hath rich gifts for thee above;
   Give of thy substance, now, in love.

3. Give to the Lord, as he has blessed thee,
   Who pours forth bounties rich and full;
   Let all thy selfish aims confessed be;
   Gain not the world, and lose thy soul!
   Put all thou hast in God's own hands,
   In trust obeying his commands. *Amen.*

JAMES BOERINGER

James Boeringer is Instructor in Music at the State University of
South Dakota and Minister of Music at Trinity Lutheran Church,
both in Vermillion, South Dakota. He was formerly Minister of
Music at the Lutheran Church of Our Savior in New York City.
He received his B.A. at the College of Wooster, Ohio, and his M.A.
at Columbia University. He is the author of one of the Society's
Youth Hymns of 1958, and is a staff writer for various musical
periodicals.

O GOD, THY HAND THE HEAVENS MADE

C.M.D.

Tune: *Forest Green* or *Shepherds' Pipes*

1. O God, thy hand the heavens made
   And all that they contain;
   The world appeared at thy command,
   And in it thou shalt reign.
   The restless sea, the land, the sky,
   Thy handiwork declare;
   The touch of thy creative pow'r
   Is present everywhere.

2. To men are given gifts divine,
   All talents thou dost send;
   Inspire us now to use them well,
   Thy Kingdom to extend.
   We hold each gift a trust from thee,
   Nor claim it as our own;
   We gratefully acknowledge, Lord,
   All things are thine alone.

3. Deliver us from selfish aims,
   True stewards we would be;
   Endow us with a deep desire
   To share with men and thee.
   A full accounting we must give,
   The Master we shall face;
   Let us approach his throne with joy
   Supported by thy grace. *Amen.*

FRANK LEROY CROSS

Frank Leroy Cross is Literary Editor of the Lorenz Publishing Company of Dayton, Ohio. He was formerly associated with the United Seminary (formerly Bonebrake Seminary) of the Evangelical United Brethren, and served from 1934 to 1946 as pastor of the First United Brethren Church, Oklahoma City, Oklahoma. He is the author of one of the Society's Bible Hymns and also one of the Society's Rural Hymns. He is a graduate of Oklahoma City University, and had theological training at Bonebrake Seminary.

GOD, WHOSE GIVING KNOWS NO ENDING

8.7.8.7.D.

Tune: *Hyfrydol* or *Austrian Hymn*

1. God, whose giving knows no ending,
   All our life is from thy store:
Nature's wonder, Jesus' wisdom,
   Costly Cross, grave's shattered door.
Gifted by thee, turn we to thee,
   Offering up ourselves in praise;
Thankful song shall rise forever;
   Gracious Donor of our days.

2. Skills and time are ours for pressing
   Toward the goals of Christ, thy Son:
Men at peace in health and freedom,
   Races joined, the Church made one.
Now direct our daily labor,
   Lest we strive for self alone;
Born with talents, make us servants
   Fit to answer at thy throne.

3. Treasure, too, thou hast entrusted,
   Gain through powers thy grace conferred;
Ours to use for home and kindred,
   And to spread the Gospel Word.
Open wide our hands in sharing,
   As we heed Christ's ageless call,
Healing, teaching and reclaiming,
   Serving thee who lovest all.

4. Lend thy joy to all our giving,
   Let it light our pilgrim way;
From the dark of anxious keeping,
   Loose us into generous day.
Then when years on earth are over,
   Rich toward thee and fellow man,
Lord, fulfill beyond our dreaming
   All our steward life began. *Amen.*

ROBERT LANSING EDWARDS

Robert Lansing Edwards is pastor of Immanuel Congregational Church, Hartford, Connecticut. He formerly served for seven years as pastor of the Congregational Church, Litchfield, Connecticut. He was graduated from Princeton University in 1937 and from Union Theological Seminary, New York, in 1949. During the intervening years, he did graduate work at Harvard University and served in the Army in World War II.

GLORIOUS IS THY NAME, MOST HOLY

8.7.8.7.D.
Tune: *In Babilone* or *Austrian Hymn*

1. Glorious is thy Name, Most Holy,
    God and Father of us all;
   We thy servants bow before thee,
    Strive to answer every call.
   Thou with life's great good hast blest us,
    Cared for us from earliest years;
   Unto thee our thanks we render;
    Thy deep love o'ercomes all fears.

2. For our world of need and anguish
    We would lift to thee our prayer.
   Faithful stewards of thy bounty,
    May we with our brothers share.
   In the name of Christ our Savior
    Who redeems and sets us free,
   Gifts we bring of heart and treasure,
    That our lives may worthier be.

3. In the midst of time we journey,
    From thy hand comes each new day;
   We would use it in thy service,
    Humbly, wisely, while we may.
   So to thee, Lord and Creator,   .
    Praise and honor we accord—
   Thine the earth and thine the heavens,
    Through all time the Eternal Word. *Amen.*

RUTH ELLIOTT

Ruth Elliott was a member of the Executive Staff of the former Board of Foreign Missions of the Presbyterian Church U.S.A. from 1921 until her retirement in 1954. During these years she has been active in many important projects and organizations including the United Stewardship Council. She is an alumna of Wellesley College, and has done graduate work at Cornell and Cambridge University, England. In her earlier years, she taught at the Northfield School for Girls.

O GOD OF LOVE, WHO GAVEST LIFE

C.M.
Tune: *Marlow* or *St. Columba*

1. O God of love, who gavest life,
   What shall we give to thee,
   Whose wealth is all the universe,
   Whose time eternity?

2. Take thou, O Lord, our humble hearts,
   Devoted to thy praise,
   Our very selves—in gratitude
   To serve thee all our days.

3. Thus we would give our precious time,
   Each dedicated hour
   To be an offering blest of thee
   To make thy church a power.

4. And all the talents that we have
   We pray thee use, O Lord,
   To magnify thy glorious name
   And spread abroad thy word.

5. So then with heart and time and skills
   All given in love to thee,
   We gladly share our earthly goods
   To bless humanity. *Amen.*

E. URNER GOODMAN

E. Urner Goodman retired a few years ago as Director of United Church Men in the National Council of Churches where he had served since its organization. Previous to that for twenty years he was National Program Director of the Boy Scouts of America. He was active in the Men and Religion Forward Movement and helped to organize the National Council of Presbyterian Men. He is the author of the hymn, "Christ Calls the Sons of Men," introduced in Church Men's Week in 1953; and also of hymns in the Society's Rural Hymns and Christian Education Hymns. Currently he is licensed as a lay speaker in the Methodist Church and preaches frequently in churches in Vermont and Florida.

THE EARTH THOU GAVEST, LORD, IS THINE

C.M.D.

Tune: *Ellacombe* or *Gerald*

1. The earth thou gavest, Lord, is thine;
   We stand on hallowed ground.
   In field and forest, mart and mine
   Thy handiwork is found.
   O Lord of earth and sky and sea,
   In this our dwelling-place
   We pledge to thee fidelity,
   Empowered by thy grace.

2. We would not claim what is not ours,
   Nor thy fair land despoil;
   We hold in trust the golden hours
   Thou givest us for toil.
   Our talents, too, of mind or hand
   Are ours by thy bequest;
   To serve mankind in every land
   We strive at thy behest.

3. Beyond the turmoil of our day
   Whose tasks are scarce begun,
   We long to hear the Master say,
   "Well done, thou faithful one!"
   O save us, Lord, from selfish greed
   From pride of stubborn will,
   As stewards both in word and deed,
   Our calling to fulfill.

4. We would not yield to false acclaim
   Or bow in craven fear;
   Above the proudest earthly name
   Thy Kingdom's goal shines clear.
   O Lord of earth and sky and sea,
   In this our dwelling-place
   We pledge to thee fidelity,
   Empowered by thy grace. *Amen.*

GEORGIA HARKNESS

Georgia Harkness is Professor of Applied Theology at the Pacific School of Religion, Berkeley, California. Until 1950 she taught theology at Garrett Biblical Institute, Evanston, Illinois, and earlier taught philosophy and religion at Elmira and Mount Holyoke Colleges. She is an ordained minister of the Methodist Church. She has given distinguished leadership in the Ecumenical Movement.

GIVER OF ALL, TO THEE WE RAISE

L.M.
Tune: *Keble* or *Duke Street*

1. Giver of all, to thee we raise
   Our grateful hymn of love and praise.
   Thine is the love that crowns our years,
   And thine the grace that stills our fears.

2. Lover of men, to thee we bring
   Our riches, worthiest offering—
   Lives unto thee in faith returned,
   Hearts high with purpose from thee learned.

3. Master of life, to thee we yield
   Full fruitage of life's harvest field—
   Words answering that great love of thine,
   Deeds thou hast prompted, Friend divine.

4. Dear Son of God, we follow thee
   To find our truest liberty;
   Thee would we serve, obey and love
   All earthborn, selfish claims above.

5. All that we have to thee we bear,
   With thee, blest Giver, all to share,
   That life abundant we may know,
   Foretaste of heaven here below. *Amen.*

Thomas Bruce McDormand

Thomas Bruce McDormand is President of Eastern Baptist Theological Seminary at Philadelphia. Through the years, he has occupied many positions of importance among Canadian Baptists, including the editorship of Canadian Baptist Sunday School Publications. He has served also as Secretary of the Baptist Federation of Canada, and is a member of the Executive Committee of the Baptist World Alliance. He is the author of several books and has published a number of poems. He has held pastorates in Middleton and Amherst, Nova Scotia, and Edmonton, Alberta.

GIVE THANKS, MY SOUL, FOR HARVEST

7.6.7.6.D.

Tune: *Llangloffan* or *Greenland*

1. Give thanks, my soul, for harvest,
   For store of fruit and grain;
   But know the Owner giveth
   That we may share again:
   Where men are lone and hungry,
   Or little children cry,
   With gifts from God's rich bounty
   May thankfulness reply.

2. Give thanks, my soul, for riches,
   Of woodland, mine, and hill;
   But know that gold and timber
   Are the Creator's still,
   Are God's on loan to stewards
   To fashion and to share,
   Providing all earth's children
   The blessing of his care.

3. Give thanks, my soul, for labors,
   That strength and days employ;
   But know the Master's purpose
   Brings toil as well as joy.
   Where leads the path to error,
   Where justice lies in chain,
   Where hoarders cause new hunger,
   There must we strive again.

4. Give thanks, my soul, for beauty,
   For dream, and hope, and plan,
   For Christ, Divine Revealer
   Of God's concern for man.
   Show forth, O God, thy purpose;
   Direct our will and hand
   To share thy love and bounty
   With men in every land. *Amen.*

WILLIAM WATKINS REID

William Watkins Reid is currently a member of the staff of the Methodist Board of Missions. Until recently he had served for many years as the Director of the Department of News Service of the Board. He has long been active in the Hymn Society, serving a term as President, and for the past few years as Chairman of the Executive Committee. His college work was done at New York University. He is the author of hymns in the Society's Rural Hymns, World Order Hymns and Christian Education Hymns.

AS MEN OF OLD THEIR FIRST FRUITS BROUGHT

C.M.D.

Tune: *Forest Green* or *Ellacombe*

1. As men of old their first fruits brought
   Of orchard, flock, and field
   To God the Giver of all good,
   The Source of bounteous yield;
   So we today first fruits would bring—
   The wealth of this good land,
   Of farm and market, shop and home,
   Of mind, and heart, and hand.

2. A world in need now summons us
   To labor, love and give;
   To make our life an offering
   To God, that man may live;
   The Church of Christ is calling us
   To make the dream come true:
   A world redeemed by Christ-like love;
   All life in Christ made new.

3. In gratitude and humble trust
   We bring our best to thee
   To serve thy cause and share thy love
   With all humanity.
   O Thou who gavest us thyself
   In Jesus Christ thy Son,
   Teach us to give ourselves each day
   Until life's work is done. *Amen.*

FRANK VON CHRISTIERSON

After serving for fifteen years as the pastor of the newly organized Trinity Community Presbyterian Church of North Hollywood, California, Frank von Christierson has recently moved to Sacramento, California, to become the pastor of a newly organized church in that city. He had formerly served a Presbyterian church in Berkeley, California, and through the years has held many important church offices in California. Born in Finland, he was brought to America as a boy of four. He is a graduate of Stanford University and San Francisco Theological Seminary. He has written one of the Society's Ecumenical Hymns and one of its Bible Hymns. He has also written another Stewardship Hymn, "Stewards of Life," which has been widely used.

114

GOD, OUR FATHER AND CREATOR

8.7.8.7.8.7.7.
Tune: *Cwm Rhondda*

1. God, our Father and Creator,
   Lord of land and sky and sea;
   From earth's poles to the Equator
   Hymns of praise ascend to thee.
   Glory, honor and thanksgiving
   Sing we to thy majesty,
   Sing we to thy majesty.

2. Thou art Giver of the harvest,
   Where is shown thy boundless love;
   Field and orchard, mine and forest
   Thine unending goodness prove.
   Glory, honor and thanksgiving
   Bring we now, O God above,
   Bring we now, O God above.

3. Teach us, Lord, the joy of giving;
   Tune our hearts to grateful praise;
   Stir us to unselfish living,
   Serving thee in all our ways.
   Glory, honor and thanksgiving
   Offer we through endless days,
   Offer we through endless days. *Amen.*

EDWARD KRUSEN ZIEGLER

Edward Krusen Ziegler is pastor of the Williamson Road Church of the Brethren, Roanoke, Virginia. This is the fifth pastorate which he has held in his denomination. In addition to his service in the pastorate, he has held important and varied posts in the Church of the Brethren: Missionary in India 1931-1939; Director of Evangelism 1951-1955; Moderator 1959-1960. He is the author of several books and one of the 250th Anniversary Hymns of his denomination.